The Science of

Financial Market
Trading

The Science of

Financial Market
Trading

Don K Mak

World Scientific
New Jersey • London • Singapore • Hong Kong

Published by

World Scientific Publishing Co. Pte. Ltd.

5 Toh Tuck Link, Singapore 596224

USA office: Suite 202, 1060 Main Street, River Edge, NJ 07661

UK office: 57 Shelton Street, Covent Garden, London WC2H 9HE

British Library Cataloguing-in-Publication Data
A catalogue record for this book is available from the British Library.

THE SCIENCE OF FINANCIAL MARKET TRADING

ISBN 981-238-252-6

Printed in Singapore.

In memory of

my sister, Mrs. Lucy Lau, who died at the age of fifty-two, from a traffic accident, and

her husband, Mr. Ignatius Y. S. Lau, who died 100 days later, at the age of fifty-five, of a heart attack which he had no history of.

Preface

There have been many books written on the financial market. While some of them do make sense, some of them are pure fantasies.

In addition, errors, misconceptions, and over-exaggerations abound in some of these books. To cite an obvious example, in a chart where price is plotted against time, an angle of 45 degrees has been employed as part of a trading plan to signify when the market is going to turn. However, by simply changing the scale of the time axis or the price axis, the same angle can be changed to an angle of different degrees. In that perspective, it would not make sense to use angles to do any forecasting.

Some books are advertised by making use of price patterns to interpret market movements. But an interpretation of patterns is rather subjective. Five analysts can come up with six interpretations, and they will come up with different interpretations a few months later, when it becomes obvious that the previous interpretations are inconsistent with the present market behavior.

Some books are more objective, and exploit indicators to forecast the market. However, they seldom explain why a certain market movement will follow, given certain signals from the indicators. An example that is not well explained is the bullish or bearish prediction that would arise depending on how some indicators diverge from prices.

In this book, we would first take a look at how some of the financial markets may not be random from a mathematical point of view. Then we will take a look at how the markets can be modeled from different scientific perspectives. A number of scientific journal papers will be cited. Interested readers should refer to those papers for details. It should be noted that scientific research is an on-going process. Understanding of the market, or any discipline for that matter, grows with new mathematical and scientific advancement. As the market deals with crowd human behavior, which is still not very well understood, it is believed that understanding of the market is still at an infancy stage.

Later chapters of the book will emphasize discussing indicators, which are quite objective, rather than patterns, which are rather subjective. Several new indicators will be designed. They are tested on theoretical waveforms before being applied on real market data. The indicators do not have arbitrary parameters as are quite often used in some conventional indicators, which need to be adjusted to suit individual markets. They are also designed to have very little time lag. Time lag is particularly important in trading, as excessive delay will produce late buy-sell signals that may translate into lost profits. Why certain market movements will follow certain indicator response will be explained. More specifically, divergences between price and certain indicator responses will be interpreted.

Some mathematics will be used. Digital signal processing and Calculus will be employed. However, the readers do not have to understand the mathematics in order to understand the description of the new indicators and how they can be applied. A number of figures are included to explain how those indicators will behave under different conditions. Computer programs of the new indicators, written in Easy Language of Omega Research's TradeStation 2000i are also included. The mathematics of the derivation of the new indicators are placed at the Appendices for the interested readers. Other mathematics included in the Appendices help to explain the basics of some of the new ideas involved. They would also guide the readers if they would like to continue doing some research themselves.

Market forecasting would have to contain certain errors. Weather forecasting has improved a lot for the last twenty years.

Can market forecasting be improved? It is not impossible. Further research needs to be performed. But it should be remembered that the human mind is competitive and adaptive. And that would be the constraint to the accuracy of forecasting.

I would like to extend special thanks to my eldest sister, Diana Mak, who is the Professor and Head of the Department of Applied Social Sciences of the Hong Kong Polytechnic University. She has provided me with continual encouragement and support in this endeavor. I would like to thank my son, Anthony, for typing part of the manuscript. And I would like to acknowledge my wife, Margaret, for her patience and tolerance throughout the long period of my working on this project.

D. K. Mak

December, 2002

Contents

Chapter 1

Introduction

We live in an interesting world. While some of the events can be controlled by us, most of the events cannot. Among all the events, while some of the outcomes are deterministic, quite a lot of them are completely random. A simple example of a completely random outcome is the throwing of an unbiased coin. It is not possible to tell *a priori* with certainty whether it is going to land head or tail. For the completely random outcome, there is not much we can do to increase its predictability. But for some of the apparently random events, are they really completely random? If we can train ourselves to be as observant as Sherlock Holmeses, can some of the apparent random acts be less random than they appear to be? Let me cite a real life example.

About ten years ago, my whole family was visiting Hong Kong. I went with my five-year-old son Anthony to an amusement park. One of the games in the park was a water squirting competition that had ten seats. Each participant had a water pistol. Water going into all the pistols would be started by an operator. Each person would aim the water at a wooden clown's mouth, which was about one meter right in front of each pistol. As water was shot into its mouth, a ball would rise up a tube, which was connected, to the mouth. The first person that managed to raise the ball to the top could win a prize. We stood there watching several games. The people who sat on the leftmost side always won. I hypothesized that water must be piping in from the left side and distributed to all the water pistols, thus the water pressure from the leftmost side was the highest, contributing to the people sitting there always won. I mentioned this conjecture to Anthony. However, we did not stay to play any game.

Back in Ottawa and a year later, we went to an annual amusement exhibition and saw a similar game. The choice of prizes included stuffed lobsters. This was the first year that the exhibition had stuffed lobsters and they were cute. My children Angela and Anthony would like to have them. Anthony immediately went to the leftmost seat and started playing. He lost. At that point, I told Anthony, "Stop playing and let me watch for a while". For the next few games, people sitting at the center seats always won. What happened was, this game had nineteen sets, much more seats than the one in Hong Kong. I figured that the water must be piping in from the center and distributed to the water pistols on both sides. I then asked Anthony to sit in the center seat. He won three out of four games. He got three small lobsters, and he could exchange two of them for a large one. The kids were happy. So was I. I have found that an apparently random game was not so random after all.

Now, can other chaotic events have some deterministic nature? And, what about the financial markets? Are they as random as they appear to be? Or, maybe, some of the markets are less random than others. Let us first take a look at who the players are in the financial market.

The financial market intrigues many people, mostly because there is money to be made, and sometimes because the trader or investor enjoys the game of trading the market. He can go long when the market climbs, or he can short when the market crashes. As long as the market moves, there is the potential of making money and having fun.

Professional traders believe that with a trading plan and a good money management, the market can be beaten. After all, there are traders who consistently make money from the market year after year. How do traders analyze the market? They usually take the fundamental approach or the technical approach or a hybrid of both. We will take a look at these approaches.

1.1 Fundamental Analysis

For individual stocks, fundamentalists look at several variables: growth in company earnings and sales, price-to-earning ratio, insider trading, etc. (Zweig 1990). For futures and options, fundamentalists look at the prime rate, loan demand, seasonal cycles, etc. (Zweig 1990). Thus, they look at the fundamental reasons why the price will change. Decisions will be made based on these reasons on a qualitative basis, or more quantitatively, using artificial intelligence programs like neural network and genetic algorithm. Most portfolio mangers purchasing individual stocks will use some kind of fundamental analysis.

1.2 Technical Analysis

Technical analysts base their buy and sell decisions on market behavior such as price and volume. They have a slogan — "the Tape Tells All" (Weinstein 1988). It simply means that all relevant information, whether it is interest rate, inflation, or company's sales revenues and earnings, etc. — the fundamentals — that are currently known are already incorporated in the price. This view, paradoxically, is quite similar to the idea of the efficient market theory, which claims that the market is random. However, while the efficient market theory claims that news about the fundamentals instantaneously affect the price, technical analysts believe that price movement can precede news as quite often, it is the anticipation of the news that move the market (Pring 1991). There is a familiar maxim, which says, "sell on good news".

Furthermore, quite often, by the time the trader hears about the news, it may be already too late to take any action. Since it is difficult to find out about the important piece of news ahead of time, all one needs to do is to follow the tape and consider market movement as a leading indication of changes in fundamentals.

In that sense, past financial data can be employed to forecast the market. Among financial data, price is considered to be the most significant, and is quite often plotted in charts where patterns are claimed to be observed.

Not only can patterns be recognized, indicators can also be calculated from the past price to hopefully give some hint as to which direction the market is heading. Pattern recognition and calculations of indicators are the two significant aspects of technical analysis (Elder 1993, Pring 1991, DeMark 1994, Weinstein 1988).

1.2.1 Pattern Recognition

Price patterns represent the price trends that are determined by interaction of buyers and sellers. Patterns can be simple or complex. Simple patterns consist of trendlines, rectangles, and triangles (Pring 1991, Elder 1993). Complex patterns can be exemplified by Elliot Wave Theory (Prechter and Frost 1990, Nelly 1990), which states that market cycles consist of three waves up and two waves down. However, recognition of patterns can be quite subjective.

1.2.2 Indicators

Indicators operate on series of past financial data. The data would consist of price, volume, etc., among which price is the most important. Quite a number of indicators have been developed, all aiming at illustrating what the market situation is, and attempting to forecast what it will be.

Indicators in financial market are equivalent to filters in electrical engineering. They are also equivalent to operators in mathematics. The operator will convolute with the financial time series to produce another function indicative of the state of the market condition. Calculation of indicators is more objective than pattern recognition. Analysts can debate about whether a triangle pattern is present or how the Elliot waves should be labeled, but they will not argue about the results of the calculation of certain indicators.

1.3 Hybrids

This is a mix of fundamental and technical analysis. The most common form is to use fundamentals to decide whether to buy or sell, and to use technical analysis to time the trades.

In this book, we will concentrate only on technical analysis, as the parameters (e.g. price) are fewer and much well defined than those of fundamental analysis. Furthermore, we will emphasize on calculating indicators on price data and will attempt to identify trend changes at an early stage.

But trading techniques aside, the most basic question that one should ask is — is the market random? We will try to answer this question in the next chapter.

Chapter 2

Is the Market Random?

One significant question that should be asked is whether financial data are random from a mathematical point of view. Just like any other data or signals, which can be electrical, acoustical, or otherwise, financial data series should be subjected to the same signal analysis procedures.

For years, traders have been claiming that the market is not random. If it were, then there would be no point in trading. Traders quite often plot market price data versus time on charts. These chartists claim they can see patterns, e.g. rectangles, triangles, etc. in these charts (Pring 1991). Each pattern is interpreted differently as the balance of power between bulls and bears. From these patterns, they would decide which direction the market is heading. However, it has been pointed out that patterns can arise out of complete randomness (Peterson 1997). On a clear night, we can see thousands of stars scattered across the sky. It is not difficult to pick out patterns like a lion or a bear from a certain group. Similarly, one can write a computer program to simulate market behavior by treating price as a random walk. A random walk is a summation of independent and identically distributed (iid) variables (Brockwell and Davis 1996). Every time the program is run, a different curve will be drawn. Quite often, we can see patterns such as triangles and rectangles in the curves. A trader can easily suggest profitable entry and exit points. This apparent regularity among randomness represents special cases from a branch of mathematics known as Ramsey theory (Peterson 1997). Ramsey theory describes the appearance of regular patterns in a large set of randomly chosen objects. The theory implies that complete disorder is impossible.

For years, academics have been saying that the market is random, and the efficient market theory holds. The efficient market theory states that market prices reflect the knowledge and expectations of all investors. Thus it is futile to forecast market movements. Any news is reflected in the company's stock price, thus making it impossible to beat the market. The efficient market theory originated from Louis Bachelier (1870-1946), who is considered to be the pioneer of all statistical approaches to finance. In 1900, Bachelier, in his Ph. D. Thesis, claimed that charting was useless and that the market was random (Mandelbrot 1983, 1997). More specifically, he wrote that the price change followed, in the first approximation, a one-dimensional Brownian motion. Brownian motion is the non-stopping irregular motion of small particles, e.g., pollen grains, held in suspension in a liquid. The motion has a normal (Gaussian) distribution. Nevertheless, Bachelier did note certain discrepancies between the financial data and his Gaussian random walk model. Firstly, the sample variance changes in time. The sample variance is the mean of the square of the variation of each sample from the mean (Meyer 1965; Freund 1992). Secondly, there are very large changes in price that cannot be accounted for. In 1963, Mandelbrot pointed out that the random price variation was actually ruled by a Levy stable distribution, which has wings larger than expected for a normal process and has an infinite variance (Mandelbrot 1983, 1997; Casti 1997a). In 1995, Mantegna and Stanley (1995) studied the S & P 500 index variations and concluded that a Levy distribution described well this random process over time intervals spanning from 1 minute to 1000 minutes. To resolve the paradox of the infinite variance, they introduced the truncated Levy flight distribution, which has a finite variance, so as to explain the unavoidable cutoff in any physical systems (Mantegna and Stanley 1994, 1995).

Whatever distribution the price variation is, the market is still a random process, which is what the efficient market theory claims. However, I believe, there is a flaw in the build-in assumption of the efficient market theory. Its basic premise implies that all investors learn of the news at the same instant, which cannot be true. There are insiders who learn of the news before they appear in public. There are professional traders who monitor the news by the minute, and there are mutual fund investors who learn of the news most likely from next day's newspaper. Even with the fast speed of the spread of information these days, there is bound to be different time lags of the news being received by the traders and investors, who will act accordingly, thus affecting the market price. Palmer et al (1994) also questioned the assumptions of the efficient market theory, and its related rational expectation theory (Jaditz and Sayers 1992). They argued that the agents do not necessarily have full knowledge of the information. Furthermore, they are not perfectly rational, and may not be able to deduce their optimum behavior. In addition, they cannot rely on others to duplicate their own logic. Different agent may receive different information about a situation, and may employ different approaches. This, then, can imply that there are certain market trends, and that the market may not be completely random.

Testing whether a data sequence is random is hampered by the fact that randomness is not a very well defined mathematical concept. Different kinds of tests have been proposed (Brockwell and Davis 1996). Each test checks the hypothesis that the data are values of independent and identically distributed (iid) random variables. The general strategy is to apply all the tests and observe whether any of them is able to detect any deviation from the iid hypothesis. If some tests are not able to detect any deviation from the iid behavior, but other tests do so quite strongly, one should consider rejecting the iid hypothesis. Tests have been performed on the Dow-Jones Utilities Index, showing that the index was not random (Brockwell and Davis 1996).

In 1991, Steven Pincus, a mathematician, introduced a new concept called approximate entropy (Pincus 1991, 1995, 1996, 1997; Stewart 1997) to evaluate randomness. The new concept yields the average unpredictability of a number, and can apply to a sequence of any length. Using this method, he has shown that changes in the values of stocks, measured by the S&P 500 index, are far from random.

In 1994, Kaplan (1994) employed a new kind of statistics to analyze the exchange rate between the Swiss Franc and the U.S. dollar. He pointed out that there existed a low frequency variability (slower than 15 minutes), and conjectured that the exchange rate was not entirely a random walk.

If the price variation of a certain market is not a random sequence, is there a reason for this? The explanation may lie in the fact that more and more traders are becoming technical analysts, i.e., they forecast the future price movement by analyzing the past price data. If so, even though each trader would have his own rules, the future would be a function of the past. This reasoning may apply to Bond and Futures market. It may not apply to markets of individual stocks, where investors and mutual fund managers are most likely fundamental analysts, i.e., their decision making would include factors like company earnings, and interest rates. In those markets, there will not be a correlation between future price and past price, as past price is not employed to make decisions.

There can be another reason why a price sequence is not random. If certain news causes a market or a stock to go downhill (or uphill) during a certain period, the price sequence during that period would be quite directional and not random.

Only if the market is not random would we be able to create mathematical models, which most likely will be probabilistic rather than deterministic. We will discuss models of the financial markets in the next chapter.

Chapter 3

Models of the Financial Market

A model, by definition, is a simplification of reality. A model must have assumptions and approximations. This simply because nature or reality is very complicated. To put a large number of factors in the model will cloud the whole issue. The essential point is to determine which factors are significant and which ones cause only perturbations. An example will be given. When a marble is dropped on the floor, we can assume that the earth's gravitational force is the only force acting on the marble, and other force, e.g. air resistance, play a very insignificant role. We can forecast, quite well when and where the marble is going to drop on the floor. Thus, the gravitational force model is a good model in this case. However, when a feather is dropped onto the floor, other forces play a more important role and need to be included in the model. Thus, model building will depend upon whether the model can explain and forecast real phenomena.

Not all models can perform both functions. They can be either explanatory or predictive (Casti 1997b). It would, of course, be best to find a model that can both explain the past and forecast the future. Good models have certain characteristics:

(1) Simplicity

A model should be as simple as possible and contains just enough terms to explain the facts. This principle can be represented by the doctrine called Ockham's Razor, which states that "entities are not to be multiplied beyond necessity".

(2) Objectivity

A model should be objective. This means that anybody anywhere in the world should arrive at the same result. Objectivity implies reproducibility.

(3) Conformity

A model should conform to well-established theories. This does not mean that well-established theories are sacred, as they may need to be corrected if new experimental evidences appear. However, well-established theories are usually very well thought of and need quite some justification to be proved incorrect.

(4) Applicability

A model will be a better model if it can explain a wider variety of phenomena that may look seemingly unrelated. An example would be the Universal Law of Gravitation, which can explain planetary motions as well as an apple falling from a tree.

(5) Agreement with experimental data

Comparison should be made between predictions of a model and the results of experiments. If the agreement is good and if it does not contain too many empirical constants adjusted to fit the data, then the model is usually endorsed. If the parameters are determined independently and then used as inputs to the model as fixed constants, one can claim a good degree of confidence in the model (Aris 1994).

(6) Non-arbitrariness

A model is a better model if it contains fewer or preferably no arbitrary parameter in its mathematical equations. Arbitrary parameters are constructed from curve fitting to existing experimental data and thus may not agree with new experimental data. A model is considered a better model if it is derived independently of experimental data. Usually, a model with no arbitrary parameter has a larger range of applicability.

Models can be mathematical or non-mathematical (Casti 1997b). We will primarily concern ourselves with only mathematical models as we are dealing with financial price data that are number series. The ABC of formulating a mathematical model has been described by Mesterton-Gibbons (1995). A is for Assume. We should boldly make assumptions where no one has assumed before. What we are given is usually not enough; we need to make up what we are lacking. B is for Borrow. We borrow ideas and theories from well-established models to interpret the new phenomena. We borrow from the familiar to explain the unfamiliar. C is for Criticize. We should rigorously criticize our model. Are the assumptions correct? Can we put old wine into new bottles? Do the calculations of our model agree with experimental data? If these questions are not satisfactorily answered, the model need to be revised, or we may need to go back to the drawing board and re-start again from scratch.

Mathematical models can be divided into deterministic and probabilistic. The behavior of a physical phenomenon can quite often be described by a model based on physical laws, which can yield accurate values of some time-dependent quantity. Such model can be classified as deterministic. An example would be models for planetary movements. In many other problems, time dependent phenomenon such as monthly sales of a company, depends on many unknown factors. It is simply not possible to derive a deterministic model to accurately calculate the future behavior of the phenomenon. However, it may be possible to come up with a model to estimate the probability of a future value lying between two specified limits. This kind of model is classified as a probability model or a stochastic model. Models for forecasting financial time series are stochastic models. Furthermore, they are kinematic rather than dynamic models, i.e., they describe how the price moves but do not explain why.

It should be noted than no phenomenon is totally deterministic. A ball dropping onto the floor can be described by gravitational force. However, unknown factors, such as wind can throw the ball off the predicted target. If we cannot forecast precisely phenomena governed by physical laws, there is no reason to believe that we can forecast precisely stochastic process.

We will now look at how the financial market is being modeled by different endeavors.

3.1 Chaos

Chaos is a system that never finds a steady state — a system that will almost repeat itself but never quite succeeds. The weather is such a system. The weather can be modeled by only a few equations, thus making it deterministic. However, because the result is very sensitive to initial conditions, its path can change dramatically, making it unpredictable (Gleick 1987; Peitgen and Richter 1988). This is described as the Butterfly Effect — the notion that a butterfly flapping its wing in Beijing can cause a hurricane next month in New York. Weather forecasts are speculative beyond a week, and are worthless beyond two. Chaotic problems have solution spaces called strange attractors, which has the important property of stability. In the long term, motion tends to return to the attractors.

In the late nineteen eighties, some scientists claimed that certain financial and economic time series exhibit chaotic behavior (Brock and Sayers 1988; Brock, Hsieh and Lebaron 1992; Chorafas 1994; Casti 1995). However, these claims of findings of chaos in economic data have been disputed. Jaditz and Sayers (1992) suggested several methodologies to analyze the data and concluded that there was no evidence of deterministic chaos in economic data. Gilmore (1992) applied a new topological approach, the close returns test, to analyze various economic time series. The test is capable of distinguishing between chaotic and other types of behavior. The test showed lack of evidence for chaos, and concluded that claims to find chaotic behavior in economic data need to be viewed skeptically.

3.2 Complexity

Complexity theory examines systems that lie in the middle ground between order and randomness (Waldrop 1992; Casti 1995). A complex system contains a number of agents. Examples of agents are drivers on highways and traders in a financial market. The agents are intelligent and adaptive. They make decisions and act on the basis of certain rules. They can modify the rules as new information arises, and they can create new rules. Each agent knows at best what a few other agents are doing. Based upon this limited information, they decide what to do next.

Hirabayashi et al (1993) modeled the complex system of stock market using threshold dynamics. Under different conditions, the model shows balanced time evolution of market price as well as crash-like behaviors.

Palmer et al (1994) also created a complex model of a stock market. The agents were allowed to learn and the system bootstrapped itself to a high order of mutual behavior. The price quite often stays close to the fundamental value, but it also shows major upward and downward deviations, corresponding to bubbles and crashes.

Thus, complexity theory can simulate market behavior quite well. However, knowing that the market is a complex system does not really help in forecasting it, or whether the trader should buy or sell at a certain point in time. Various approaches in helping traders to make decision as well as forecasting have been attempted. These include the wave model, time series analysis, neural network, fractal geometry, fuzzy logic, and wavelet analysis.

3.3 Wave Model

In nature, many objects vibrate or oscillate and generate waves. Examples of waves are ocean waves, earthquake waves, and sound waves in air. Not only mechanical systems can oscillate; nonmechanical systems can also do so. Radio waves, microwaves, and visible light are examples of oscillating electric and magnetic fields.

The market represents the emotions of traders who oscillate between optimism and pessimism. Thus, it will not be surprising that the wave model in nature was borrowed to explain the fluctuations of the price data.

Charles Dow observed that a rising market moves in a series of waves, each rally and correction being higher than its predecessor. When the series of rising peaks and valleys was interrupted, a trend reversal was signaled. Dow likened this phenomenon to the ripples of a wave on seashore. The Dow theory was first published in 1900 (Pring 1991).

In the 1930's, Ralph Elliott claimed that the financial market unfolded according to a basic pattern of five waves up and three waves down. Each pattern, he pointed out, is part of a larger pattern and each pattern, in turn, is made up of many smaller patterns (Prechter and Frost 1990, Neely 1990, Beckman 1992).

Plummer (1990) commented that the pattern of five waves up and three waves down is incompatible when applying to foreign exchange markets. A five-three pattern for one currency in a certain cross-rate becomes a three-five pattern for the other currency in that cross-rate. He proposed that the pattern should be three waves up and three waves down.

It should be noted that the labeling of these waves is highly subjective. Different technical analysts would label the waves quite differently. Furthermore, a technical analyst would re-label the waves after a few months, when it became obvious that the original labeling was incompatible with the present market patterns. These wave models are quite simple. However, because of its subjectivity, these models are not good scientific models.

Market waves can also be viewed in the most basic pattern — one wave up and one wave down, which constitutes a cycle. To find a cycle is to measure the time between the same phase on successive cycles. The resultant measurement is the period of a simple cycle. A cycle finder can be as simple as a ruler, or as complicated as the Maximum Entropy Spectral Analysis (MESA) as proposed by Ehlers (1992). The MESA approach is a variation of deconvolution filtering techniques. When convoluted with the original signal, the filter outputs a white noise with a constant spectrum at all frequencies. MESA is a rather objective method of finding a cycle. It requires about one cycle's worth of input data.

However, market data shows that the length of a cycle changes quite often. The wave does not usually last even one cycle. Thus, more importantly, instead of attempting to find the cycle, we would like to know when the market is going to turn. In this book, we will describe a new indicator, the velocity indicator, which will require only about a quarter of a cycle of data to forecast which direction the market is heading. Since the velocity indicator has a very small phase lag, it can time market turn quite well. Furthermore, the same indicator will signal whether the market is in a trending mode.

3.4 Time Series Analysis

Financial market prices are quite often plotted versus time on charts. Market price is thus an example of a time series. Prediction of time series is a problem we encounter in the study of natural phenomena, social and economic events, or human behavior. When we are given the knowledge about the past behavior of a system, can we make meaningful prediction about its future?

In some fairly stable situations, e.g., orbits of planets and satellite, their calculations are so accurate that people forget they are forecasts. However, many complex systems manifest the aspect of sensitive dependence to initial conditions, and this renders long-term predictability a hopeless task. In spite of that, some sort of predictability may be possible in the short run and this may be sufficient for adaptive systems interacting with an external environment. Short-term predictability will embody the new information as it arrives at each new time step. Given a certain number of elements of a time series the next element will be forecasted.

Several approaches that have been employed to deal with the problem of prediction of time series have been summarized by Santana and Mendes (1992). The approaches include autoregressive model, neural network and prediction of band limited functions. The first two methods will be discussed in more detail later. The last method makes use of the Shannon's sampling theorem, which states that a function for which the circular frequency vanishes outside the band $[-\omega, \omega]$ can be exactly reconstructed from its values at discrete times separated by the sampling period $T = \pi/\omega$. T^{-1} is called the Nyguist rate. As long as the sampling rate is larger than the Nyguist rate, then the signal can be reconstructed from the past samples. A high pass filter with stop band edge ω is selected from a large collection of filters, such that the output of the signal after filtering becomes negligible. From the characteristics (finite impulse response) of the filter, the one step ahead forecast can be estimated.

The drawback of the method is the requirement to have a good estimate of the frequency band in the time series. Santana and Mendes (1992) have devised a method that, at each time step, will search for the optimal bandwidth for the prediction filter. The method was applied to the inflation in Portugal in the period between January 1984 and November 1990, as well as to the sunspot number time series from 1850 to 1890. The forecasts agreed reasonably well with future data.

The most common approach to time series analysis is the autoregressive integrated moving average (ARIMA) process. The detail will be discussed in Appendix 1. One hundred successive observations of the daily IBM stock prices for a period beginning in May 1961 was fitted to the ARIMA model (Box, Jenkin and Reinsel 1994, p98). The result showed that the price series was random, and the best forecast of the future values of the stock was very nearly today's price. The ARIMA model was also used to fit the daily closing price of the Dow-Jones Utilities Index between Aug 28 and Dec 18, 1972 (Brockwell and Davis 1996, p141). The result implied that the Index was not random and was thus forecastable.

The daily closing price of the S & P index over the course of the year 1992 has been modeled with an ARIMA (8 0 0) process (Hatamian 1995). The next day index was forecasted. The forecast error averages around 2.5 S&P points. Hatamian concluded that the results were not spectacular and were not useful for trading. However, it should be noted that '8', the number of past values used was chosen rather intuitively. A more systematic estimation may produce a better result (Brockwell and Davis, 1996, p381). Hatamian later applied a nonlinear system to model the S & P Index, producing a better result of forecasting with an average error of 2.0 S&P points (Hatamian 1996). He concluded that the index might not be that random.

3.5 Neural Network

Neural network can perform intelligent mathematical operations. It consists of several layers of neurons, which are named after human brain cells. The first layer is the input neurons, which are the input data. In financial market, the input data can be interest rate, selected indicator values, etc. The hidden neurons learn how to combine the inputs to produce the desired results. The output neurons present the results. Results can be the closing values of the next day's S & P index or IBM stock price.

A neural network is trained by repeatedly presenting examples that include both inputs and outputs. The network learns from each example and calculates an output. If the output does not agree with the target output, the network will be corrected by changing its internal connections. Some connections will be strengthened and others weakened. This training will be continued until the network reaches a desired level of accuracy. New input data can then be fed into the network, which will predict whatever it is trained to do. Neural network has been proposed to forecast the market (Fishman et al. 1991, Sherald and Ward 1994).

One problem with financial neural networks is that there are many numeric parameters that can be chosen as input data. Quite a number of these parameters, especially indicators, are slight variations of each other, and therefore redundant. However, genetic algorithm, which is used to solve optimization problem, can help to sort out which parameters are significant. They employ the methods of evolution, and especially the principle of the survival of the fittest. The less fit parameter will die, and the most fit parameter will be selectively bred. After many generations of selection, the most fit parameters will remain to be the optimal solution (Chorafas 1994).

An interesting competition in forecasting time series was organized by the Complex Systems Summer School at the Santa Fe Institute in the summer of 1990 (Weigend and Gershenfeld 1994). One of the six data sets provided was the current exchange data rate between the Swish franc and the U.S. dollar. Weigend and Gershenfeld noted that a review in 1990 regarding attempts to forecast foreign rates concluded that no method had succeeded in beating the random walk hypothesis out-of-sample. However, the data employed was daily or weekly data. It was hoped that the high frequency "tick-by-tick" data available for the competition might reveal some hidden deterministic feature. Unfortunately, after employing neural network to train the data, the competitors showed that all out-of-sample predictions were on average worse than chance.

3.6 Fractal Geometry

In financial price time series, it is virtually impossible to distinguish a daily price record from, e.g., a weekly record, when the axes are not labeled (Ehlers 1992). This kind of time series is called self-similar. Self-similarity entails that the distributions of variations across lags of size k have a scaling behavior characterized by the fractal dimension D.

In 1963, Mandelbrot (1983) showed that cotton prices have self-similarity, and introduced Levy distributions in the modeling of price records. The fractal dimension, D, was found to be 1.7. Evertsz (1995) also found self-similarity in the 30 German stock (DAX) index which has a fractal dimension of 1.46 (Valdez-Cepeda and Solano-Herrera 1999).

Fractal Geometry was also employed by Valdez-Cepeda and Solano-Herrera (1999) to analyze the distribution of the daily close of five financial indexes, for a period of about 500 days each. However, they assumed that the average variances were related to the time increments by a power law. This assumption implies that the process is self-affine, i.e., different coordinate scale at different rates, which is different from the self-similar process, where different coordinate scale at the same rate. An example of a self-affine process is the Brownian motion. If the time scale is rescaled by a factor "b" and the length scale is rescaled by a factor "b $^{1/2}$", the original distribution is reproduced. The fractal dimension D of the financials indexes were estimated. The industrial Dow-Jones index is described by a D = 1.332 ± 0.11, reflecting the significance of long-range (trend) variation. D of the German DAX Composite index is estimated to be 1.688 ± 0.026, implying that it is dominated by short-range variations. British Footsie (D = 1.495 ± 0.009) and the Australian Share Price (all ordinaries) (D = 1.506 ± 0.008) indexes behave like the Brownian motion (D = 1.5), The Nikkei Cash index is described by a D = 1.474 ± 0.008, implying that the short-range variation is almost as significant as the long-term variation. The D of the DAX index is different from the D value of 1.46 found by Evertsz (1995). The quantitative difference can be explained since Evertsz employed the model of self-similarity instead of self-affinity to estimate D, as well as a larger and different total number of business days.

3.7 Fuzzy Logic

Fuzzy logic rests on the idea that things usually are not crisply defined. There is usually a certain vagueness in the description of qualities (McNeill and Freiberger 1993). Thus, a person is not either tall or short. There is a range of grades between the two extremes. Fuzzy logic is the way that human brain functions. It is quite different from classical logic, which declares that a statement can only be either true or false.

Fuzzy logic can be used to analyze certain situations. Its analysis method works as such: (1) input data are described as a large number of fuzzy perceptions, (2) the inputs are processed according to a string of fuzzy if-then rules, (3) the outputs from the individual rules are weighted and averaged as a "center of mass" and condensed into one single output decision.

Fuzzy logic was first proposed by Prof. Lotfi Zadeh of the University of California at Berkeley in 1965 (McNeill and Freiberger 1993), and has since been applied to controls of automatic transmission, air conditioning and subway's running and braking system (Sowell 1998). It has also been applied to financial analysis (Chorafas 1994, Sowell 1998). For financial analysis, inputs can include price earnings ratio, cash flow etc. A number of if-then rules are created to give an assessment value to each input. Each input factor is given a weight that varies from 0 to 1.0. An input factor that is highly important will be weighted as 1 and less important factor will be weighted less. The product of assessment value and weight from all inputs are averaged and compared with a pre-determined rule to decide whether to buy or sell. This fuzzy logic decision-making method removes the personal emotion and irrationality.

3.8 Wavelet analysis

Wavelet analysis is essentially a refinement of Fourier analysis. Fourier, a French mathematician and physicist, discovered that every signal, no matter how complicated it is, could be reproduced as a sum of sine waves. However, Fourier analysis does not deal well with signals of short duration. Its representation of a localized signal requires a large number of Fourier components.

Wavelet analysis, a mathematical technique that was introduced in the 1980's, employs generalized local base functions called wavelets that can be stretched and translated with a flexible resolution in both time and frequency. The flexible windows narrow while focusing on high-frequency signals but widens while looking for low-frequency signals. As such, abrupt changes can be located in time quite precisely (Baeyer 1995; Lau and Weng 1995; Hubbard, 1998).

Studies using wavelet transform techniques applied to financial markets have been summarized by Ramsey (1999) and Shin and Han (1999). Some studies used wavelets to decompose any signal into its time-scale components. Different behavior can occur in different time scales (Ramsey and Lampart 1998 a & b). For example, in the financial market, some traders buy and hold securities for years, and thus concentrate on the market fundamentals while other traders trade on a much shorter time-scale and are interested in deviations of the market from its long-term growth. The S&P 500 index from January 1928 to June 1990 was examined by Ramsey et al (1995) using wavelet analysis. The actual data used was the growth rate of the S&P 500 index, which is defined as

$$r(n) = \frac{x(n) - x(n-1)}{x(n-1)} \qquad (3.1)$$

where x(n) represents the daily price of the S&P 500 index.

They plotted the amplitudes of wavelet coefficients for different frequencies versus time. The wavelet coefficient is the projection of the data onto the analyzing wavelet of various scaling. By varying the time with the zoom level changing from 2^5 to 2^0 , a series of six graphs were plotted. They found self-similarity in the plots. Self-similarity (or scale invariance) means that the system has no characteristic scale; the description of the system is the same at all time scales. This result led to the conclusion that there might be some predictability in the data.

A different wavelet approach, the technique of thresholding, has been employed by other researchers. Wavelet coefficients, whose absolute values are smaller than a fixed threshold, are eliminated. The remaining coefficients are then used to reconstruct the signal, thus minimizing the error of approximation. This technique is also called denoising or wavelet shrinkage. Neural network (Shin and Han 1999) or time series analysis (Capobianco 1999) has been applied to the reconstructed signal to forecast the next value. It was shown that the root mean square error of the forecasted value from the actual value was smaller for the reconstructed signal when compared to that of the original signal. This shows substantial potential to the wavelet approach.

The wavelet approach has the flexibility in handling very irregular data series. It has the capability to represent highly complex structures even though the underlying functional form is not known. The potential provided by wavelets to analyze financial price data is readily apparent. We will come back to wavelet analysis in Chapter 9.

Chapter 4

Signals and Indicators

This book is about the financial market, but it interprets the market in scientific and mathematical terms. The reason is simple. Quite a number of scientific and mathematical concepts are well established, while some of the financial market concepts are rather evasive. When one reads some books on trading rules on the market, one wonders what is the rationale behind some of these ideas, if there is any at all. Science, generally, can be employed to explain different phenomena. Financial market data, just like any data, can be subjected to scientific and mathematical findings. There is, therefore, no reason why some of the scientific ideas cannot be used to clarify some of the market concepts.

What exactly is a signal in scientific terms? A signal is any physical quantity that changes with time, distance, or any independent variable. A signal depends very much on the tool that we use to extract information from the object under investigation. Given a piece of metal, we can use X-ray or ultrasound or others as a measurement tool. The signal obtained would yield different information about the quality of the metal. The signal originally detected is called raw signal, and it can further be processed to yield information that is hidden and unclear. In the financial market, a raw signal can be the price of commodity futures contracts, or its volume traded in a particular period, or others. A raw signal or a processed signal is a dependent variable; its changes depending on the changes of an independent variable, which is usually taken to be time in the financial market. What technical analysts would like to see is what predicament they can draw from processing the raw signal or data from the market. In general, as money is the bottom line of any trade, price is the most important raw signal that they would process and analyze.

Taking time to be the independent variable, a signal can be considered as a time-varying process. A signal continuous with respect to time is called a continuous-time signal or an analog signal. If it is a function of an integer-valued time variable, n, it is called a discrete-time signal or a digitized signal (Lyons 1997, Hayes 1999). Discrete-time signals are often derived by sampling a continuous-time signal, with an analog-to-digital converter. However, a signal can be a discrete-time signal to start with. An example is the tick data in the financial market. A tick is the upward or downward price movement in a security's trade. There can be, e.g., 10 tick data within one minute of trading. To condense all these information, tick data are quite often sampled within a predetermined time interval. For example, in a 10-minute chart, the price of the opening tick and the closing tick, as well as the highest and lowest tick during every 10-minute interval are plotted in the chart. This particular way of plotting data in the financial market differs from that of other disciplines where the closing value in a certain time period is usually taken. This is because traders believe that the high, low, open and close prices do contribute some information with regard to the market activity. In an hourly chart, again, all these four prices are plotted within every hourly interval. In general, the closing prices are more often used to be the raw data. Occasionally, the average of the high and low prices is taken. However, taking the closing prices are more convenient. Furthermore, it is consistent with the mathematical concept of sampling, as, e.g., the closing price of the hourly chart can be obtained by sampling every sixth point of the closing prices of the 10-minute chart.

In 1807, a French mathematician Joseph Fourier showed that any practical signal can be expressed as the sum of a number of sine waves. This summation has been called the Fourier series (Broesch 1997, Hubbard 1998). This theorem would allow us to rewrite any financial data as a sum of sine waves. An example of a single sine wave with two cycles and an amplitude of 1.0 is shown in Fig. 4.1. A single sine wave is a sine wave with a single frequency. The sine wave is sampled at thirty-two points per cycle. Thus, the (sampling) period of the sine wave is 32 points. The (sampling) frequency, which is defined as 1/period, equals to 1/32. Since each cycle is equivalent to 2π radians (which is equal to 360 degrees, the angle subtended by a circle), the (sampling) circular frequency is $2\pi/32$ or $\pi/16$ radian. Figure 4.2 shows the summation of two sine waves, one with a circular frequency of $\pi/4$ with an amplitude of ¼ and the other with a circular frequency of $\pi/16$ with an amplitude of 1.0 .

To accurately reproduce a signal, the Nyquist theorem (Brigham 1974, Broesch 1997) states the signal has to be sampled at a rate greater than twice the frequency of the highest frequency component existing in the signal, i.e., the number of sampling points per cycle has to be more than two for the highest frequency. This is equivalent to saying that the sampling circular frequency for the highest frequency has to be smaller than π radians.

The sampling signal, **x**, can be written as

$$\mathbf{x} = (- x(N-1), x(N), x(N+1), - x(-1), x(0), x(1), x(2), -) \quad (4.1)$$

For real time applications (as in the financial market), where no future data is available, the signal **x** will be written as

$$\mathbf{x} = (- x(N-1), x(N), x(N+1), - x(-1), x(0)) \quad (4.2)$$

In the financial market, the most common signal is price, which is usually plotted as bars on a chart in a certain timeframe. As technical analysts believe that price is the most important data in market forecasting, this raw price data is processed and may be even further processed to yield any hidden information. Many manipulations or indicators have been created to predict the market's direction. Most indicators can be considered as systems in digital

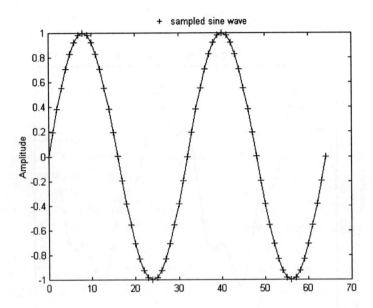

Fig. 4.1. A single sine wave of amplitude 1.0 with a circular frequency of π/16, i.e., it is sampled at thirty-two points per cycle.

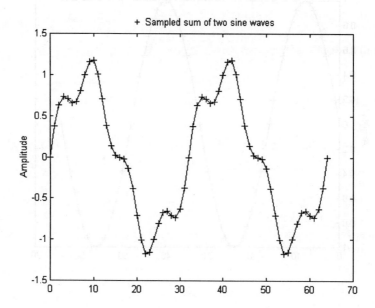

Fig. 4.2.   A summation of two sine waves, one with a circular frequency of $\pi/4$ with an amplitude of ¼ and the other with a circular frequency of $\pi/16$ with an amplitude of 1.0 .

signal processing, or operators in mathematics, or filters in electrical engineering. Once we understand this relationship, it means that we can transfer the knowledge from other fields to understand the properties of old indicators, as well as to create new indicators. Further explanation of systems is given in Appendix 2. An indicator is basically an operator or mapping that transforms an input signal to an output signal by means of a fixed set of rules. The output signal would hopefully expose certain hidden features in the original input signal. The indicator should be tested on theoretical waveforms like sine waves before applying on real market data. This procedure is usually not performed on financial market indicators.

Some of the most popular financial market indicators are actually convolution sum whose output, y(n), is related to the input, x(n) by

$$y(n) = h(0)x(n) + h(1)x(n-1) + h(2)x(n-3) + —$$ (4.3)

where h(k), k = 0, 1, 2, — is the indicator coefficient.

What makes a good indicator? An indicator, like any idea or concept in our daily life, is created such that it should serve certain pragmatic purpose. It should be clear what assumptions have been made and under what condition does the concept not apply. To give an example, the concept 'weight' is used to measure the heaviness of an object. Weight is affected by gravitational pull. Thus, the weight of an object measured on the horizon would be larger than that of the same object when it is measured on Mount Everest. Objects are weightless in outer space as the earth is too far away to exert any gravitational pull. If someone makes up a rule saying that the cost of an object of a certain material should be proportional to the weight of the object, then he should understand that the weight varies somewhat with respect to altitude, and that the rule would not apply in outer space. If he would like his rule to apply to all conditions, he would have to look for a different concept, if it exists. In this particular case, he can change his rule to say that the cost should be proportional to mass, as mass of an object is independent of any gravitational pull. (In Physics, mass is defined as weight divide by acceleration due to gravitational pull). Thus, a good indicator should be an indicator that should apply to all or at least most of the situations of interest, and the conditions that it does not apply should be clearly defined and known before hand. This, unfortunately, is rarely the case with indicators of market data. Let us take a look at two examples.

4.1 Stochastic Indicator

The first example is stochastic, an indicator which is quite popular with traders. The word stochastic here has a completely different meaning from the probabilistic meaning as described in Chapter 3. The indicator is somehow called stochastic by chance (Ehlers 1992). Stochastic compares the current closing price with the latest high and the latest low in a time window or interval chosen by the trader (Pring 1991, Ehlers 1992, Elder 1993). Examples of time window are 10 minutes, a day, etc. Stochastic, K, is defined as

$$K = (C - L)/(H - L) \qquad (4.4)$$

where C = closing price of the current bar
   H = the highest price in the chosen time window
   L = the lowest price in the chosen time window.

Stochastic is therefore not a convolution sum as described in Eq (4.3). It is a normalized function that varies between zero and one. It can be considered as a high pass filter that filters off very low frequency. We will take a look and see how the chosen time window will affect the behavior of the stochastic.

Imagine a market in a cycle mode and the data being simulated is a single sine wave with a period of 64 points (Fig. 4.3(a)), and choose the time window to be the same as the period of the sine wave. The stochastic would have the same shape as the input data,, but swings between zero and one (Fig. 4.3(a)). As such, it does not have any time lag from the input data, which will make it

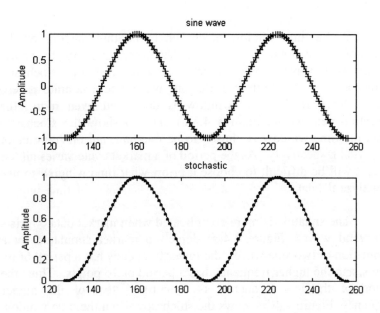

Fig. 4.3(a). The top figure shows a single sine wave, and the bottom figure shows its stochastics whose time window equals the period of the sine wave.

perfect for timing turning points. If the time window is chosen to be more than one period, the stochastic would still have the same output response. However, if the high and low of the preceding cycle are different from those of the current cycle, which usually happens in real market situation, the output response would differ in shape from the input response, causing timing errors.

If the time window is chosen to be three-quarter of the period of the input sine wave, the stochastic corresponding to the top of the sine wave would saturate at one, and the stochastic corresponding to the bottom of the sine wave would saturate at zero (Fig. 4.3(b)). If the time window is decreased even more, the saturation gets worse. Figures 4.3(c) and (d) show the stochastic when the time window is chosen to be one-half and one-quarter of the period respectively. As the period of a market cycle varies all the time, it will be difficult to choose a priori what time window to use to analyze the data.

The situation is more complicated when market data consists of several waves. Figure 4.4(a) depicts a market simulated by a summation of two sine waves, the lower frequency has a period of 64 points, and the higher frequency has a period of 16 points. Thus, the period of the low frequency is four times that of the higher frequency. Figure 4.4(b) shows the stochastic when the time window is chosen to be the period of the lower frequency. The stochastic has the same shape as the market data. When the time window is chosen to be half the period of the lower frequency, as in Fig. 4.4(c), the stochastic corresponding to the top and bottom of the waves saturate. A bearish divergence thus occurs at the top, as prices rally to a new high but stochastic does not trace a higher high. Divergence between indicator and price is considered a powerful trading rule by traders. But it should be noted that in this case, divergence occurs only when the time window is chosen to be less than the period of the lower frequency. As the existence of divergence depends very much on the time window one chooses, its implication remains doubtful. In general, as we do not know how many waves are in the market, and what frequencies they are at, the choice of the time window would be difficult. Thus, the usefulness of stochastic as an indicator is limited.

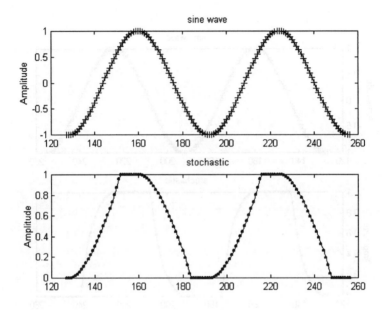

Fig. 4.3(b). The top figure shows a single sine wave, and the bottom figure shows its stochastics whose time window equals three-quarter of the period of the sine wave.

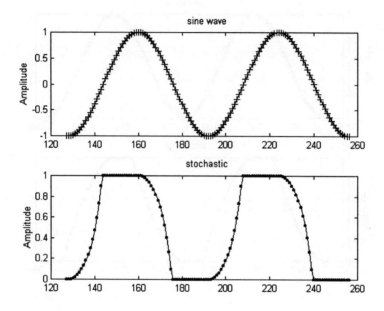

Fig. 4.3(c). The top figure shows a single sine wave, and the bottom figure shows its stochastics whose time window equals half the period of the sine wave.

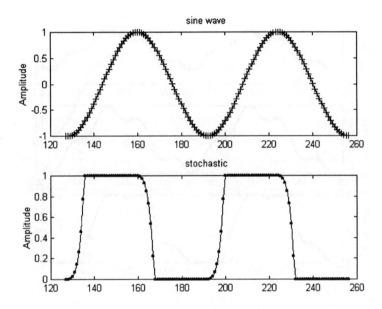

Fig. 4.3(d). The top figure shows a single sine wave, and the bottom figure shows its stochastics whose time window equals one quarter of the period of the sine wave.

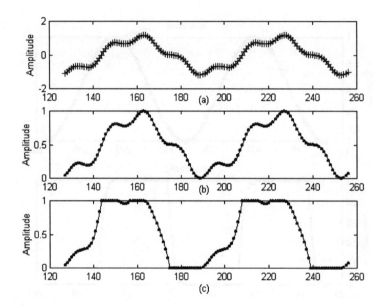

Fig. 4.4(a) The sum of two sine waves, the lower frequency has a period which is four times the period of the high frequency; (b) stochastics of the sum of the two sine waves, with time window equal to the period of the lower frequency; (c) stochastics of the sum of the two sine waves, with time window equal to half the period of the lower frequency.

4.2 Momentum Indicator

Another example is the momentum indicator, which is quite popular with traders. Momentum indicator is usually defined as the difference in successive price values (Pring 1991, Ehlers 1992, Elder 1993). It is, therefore, an example of a convolution sum as described in Eq (4.3), with h(0) equals 1 and h(1) equals −1. Momentum is defined as:

$$y(n) = x(n) - x(n-1) \qquad (4.5)$$

where y(n) is the momentum of the nth bar
    x(n) is the closing price of the nth bar
    x(n-1) is the closing price of the bar before the nth bar.

Momentum represents a simplification of the rate of change. (Rate of change is called derivative in Calculus). According to technical analysts, a strong momentum would mean that the market is trending, and a weak momentum would imply that a turning point may not be too far ahead. However, for an indicator to be useful, it should truly represent the property that it attempts to depict, and with no time delay. This is not the case with momentum, which lags behind the real rate of change for about half the time interval between adjacent bars. In Fig. 4.5, market price data is modeled as a sine wave. Its rate of change is a cosine wave (as can be shown in Calculus) plotted also in the figure. Cosine wave leads a sine wave by $\pi/2$ radians (or 90 degrees). As noted in the figure, the zero points of the cosine waves correspond to the turning points of the sine wave. This simply implies that zero points of the rate of change of a curve could identify when the curve is going to turn. However, this property has not been exploited by technical analysts. Part of the reason may be that there is no good indicator which actually represents the real rate of change. The best candidate so far, momentum, actually lags behind the real rate of change. This can be seen in Fig. 4.5, where momentum, as calculated from Eq (4.5) is plotted. This time lag originates from the definition of momentum.

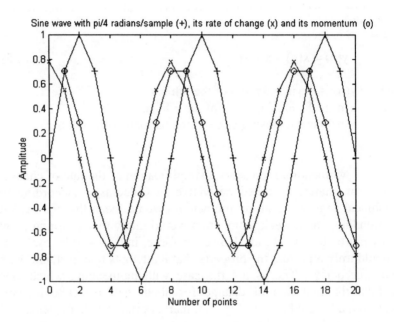

Fig. 4.5. A single sine wave (marked as +) of amplitude 1.0 with a circular frequency of $\pi/4$ radian (or 45 degrees). Its rate of change (or derivative) (marked as x) and its momentum (marked as o) are also drawn. Note that the momentum lags behind the rate of change.

The definition implies that the market is piecewise linear. However, the market should be treated as piecewise non-linear. Linearity is only a particular case of non-linearity. We will attempt to model the market as piecewise non-linear and amend the function of momentum in Chapter 6.

Most indicators can be divided into trending indicators and oscillator indicators. Examples of these indicators will be described in detail in the next two chapters.

Chapter 5

Trending Indicators

Trending indicators can help to identify trends. They are actually equivalent to low pass filters in electrical engineering. The low pass filter removes high frequency components and allows low frequency components to pass. In that sense, a trending indicator smoothes the input data. As the smoothing action employs only past data, the filtered output is delayed in phase (or time) relative to the input. Thus the trending indicators are lagging indicators; they turn after the trends reverse. If we want to decrease the lag, the output becomes less smooth. Smoothness and time or phase lag are contradictory properties. Several indicators, with different degrees of smoothness and phase lag have been developed by traders.

5.1 Simple Moving Average (SMA)

Simple moving average is by far the most common. A 7-day moving average shows the average price for the last 7 days, i.e., the prices of the last 7 days are added together and divided by 7. For the general case, an N-bar moving average is calculated by adding the prices over the last N bars and dividing by N. A bar represents a unit time interval being chosen by the trader, e. g., 1 day, 1 hour, 15 minutes, etc. SMA is called moving as the next bar's weighted price will be added to the average and the first bar's weighted price will be discarded. N is called the length of the simple moving average. A larger N will show a smoother average but a larger phase (or time) lag. Figure 5.1 shows a 15-minute chart of the US 30-year Treasury

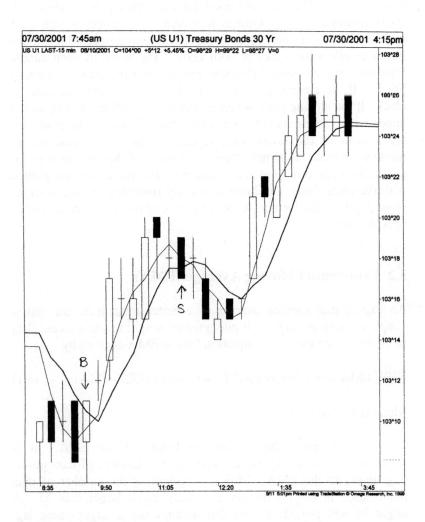

Fig. 5.1. A 15-minute chart of the US 30-year Treasury Bond Future. A simple moving average of the closing price of length 3 (thin line) and length 6 (thick line) are plotted with the price data. *Chart produced with Omega Research TradeStation2000i.*

Bond Future.   The software used for the charting is TradeStation 2000i manufactured by Omega Research.   The prices within a 15 minutes interval is plotted as a Japanese candlestick, which looks like a candle with wicks at both ends.   The body of each candle represents the absolute difference between the opening and closing prices.   If the closing price is lower than the opening, the body is black.   If the closing price is higher, the body is white.   The tip of the upper wick represents the high within the 15 minutes interval, and the bottom of the lower wick represents the low within the 15 minutes interval.   A simple moving average of the closing price of length 3 (sma3, thin line) and length 6 (sma6, thick line) are plotted with the price data.   The latter is slightly smoother and has a larger phase lag than the former.   Characteristics of the SMA are described in Appendix 3.

5.2 Exponential Moving Average (EMA)

An exponential moving average is a better trend indicator than a simple moving average as it puts greater weight to most recent data more than older data. The equation for the EMA is given by

$$\text{NEW EMA} = \alpha \times (\text{NEW PRICE}) + (1 - \alpha) \times (\text{OLD EMA}) \qquad (5.1)$$

where $\alpha = 2/(M + 1)$

M is quite often called the length of the EMA.   It is sometimes described by some traders as the number of data points (e.g. days) in the EMA.   This is incorrect as the number of data points used in the calculation is usually much larger than M.   A larger M will provide a smoother average but a larger phase lag. Figure 5.2 shows a 15-minute chart, which contains the same price data as those in Fig. 5.1.   The closing prices were smoothed by an exponential moving average of length 3 (ema3, thin line) and 6 (ema6, thick line).   The latter is smoother and has a larger phase lag than the former.   Characteristics of the EMA are described in Appendix 3.

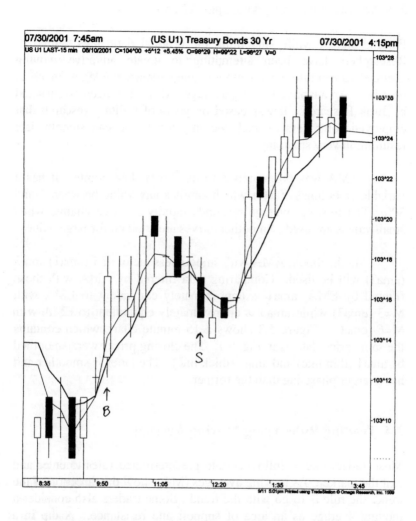

Fig. 5.2. A 15-minute chart of the US 30-year Treasury Bond Future. An exponential moving average of the closing price of length 3 (thin line) and length 6 (thick line) are plotted with the price data. *Chart produced with Omega Research TradeStation2000i.*

5.3 Adaptive Moving Average (AMA)

Filtered signal, while smoothing the original data, lags behind it. Researchers have been attempting to create adaptive moving averages to increase the smoothness and decrease the lag as much as possible. An adaptive moving average (AMA) has been constructed by Jurik Research. It was based on years of military research that employed computers to track moving targets. It can smooth data resulting in very small lag.

AMA was programmed to use thirty data points. It has a variable smoothness factor which can has any value between 1 and 500. The moving average responds rapidly to price change when small values are used. Smoother curves are attained for large values.

In this book, AMA with smoothness factor of 1 (ama1) and 3 (ama3) will be used. Comparing data filtered by AMA with those filtered by EMA, ama1 is approximately equivalent to EMA with M=3 (ema3) while ama3 is approximately equivalent to EMA with M=6 (ema6). Figure 5.3 shows a 15-minute chart, which contains the same price data as in Fig. 5.1. The closing prices were smoothed by ama1 (thin line) and ama3 (thick line). The latter is smoother and has a larger phase lag than the former.

5.4 Trading Rules using Moving Averages

Most traders like to follow certain predetermined rules to enter and exit the market. As moving averages (MA) show the direction of the trend, the rule is to go with the trend. Some traders also consider a moving average as an area of support and resistance. A dip in a rising market often finds support in an MA and turns up. A rally in a falling market often reverses when it meets resistance in an MA and turns down. Traders using MA to trade the market have constructed several trading rules:

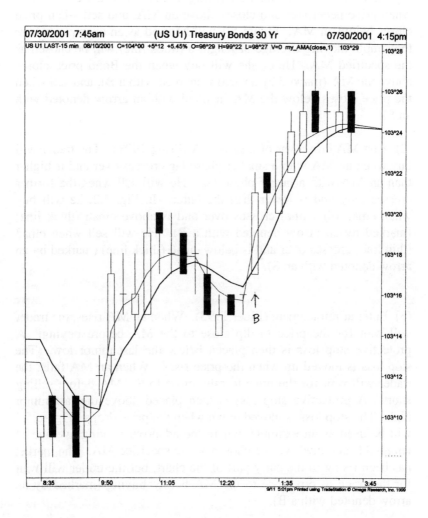

Fig. 5.3. A 15-minute chart of the US 30-year Treasury Bond Future. An adaptive moving average of the closing price of smoothness 1 (thin line) and smoothness 3 (thick line) are plotted with the price data. *Chart produced with Omega Research TradeStation2000i.*

(1) Price crossover of an MA (Pring 1991). The trader will buy when price penetrates and closes above an MA, and sell when price closes below an MA. Figure 5.1 will be used as an example, where the simple moving average of length 6 (thick line) will be chosen as the specified MA. He or she will buy when the Bond price closes above the MA (marked by an arrow denoted with a B), and sell when the price closes below the MA (marked with an arrow denoted with an S).

(2) Fast MA crossover of a slow MA (Pring 1991). The trader will buy when an MA with a smaller phase lag crosses over and is higher than an MA with a larger phase lag. He will sell when the former crosses over and is lower than the latter. In Fig. 5.2, he will buy when ema3 (thin line) crosses over and is above ema6 (thick line) (marked by an arrow denoted with a B). He will sell when ema3 (thin line) crosses over and is below ema6 (thick line) (marked by an arrow denoted with an S).

(3) Enter at retracement (Elder 1993). When an MA rises, the trader will wait for the price to dip close to the MA before buying. A protective stop loss is then placed below the last minor low. The stop loss is moved up when the price rises. When an MA falls, the trader will wait for the price to rally close to the MA before selling short. A protective stop loss is then placed above the last minor high. The stop loss is moved down when the price drops. Figure 5.3 will be used as an example, where the adaptive moving average of length 3 (thick line) will be chosen as the specified MA. The market has been rising in the early part of the chart, but the trader will wait for the price to dip close to the MA before buying (marked by an arrow denoted with a B).

The above trading rules do work some of the time. But as a market is quite unpredictable and contains whipsaws, these trading rules can also fail some of the time.

Chapter 6

Oscillator Indicators

A different kind of indicators from the trending indicators that are discussed in the last chapter is oscillator indicators. Oscillator indicators are actually equivalent to high pass filters in electrical engineering. The high pass filter removes low frequency components and allows high frequency components to pass. Thus, they measure rate of change of price over a given period of time. A common oscillator indicator is the momentum, which is defined as the subtraction of past price from present price (Pring 1991). Rising momentum is interpreted as a bullish factor and declining momentum as a bearish one.

Oscillator indicators have been used mainly in two different manners. Firstly, they can be used to estimate whether the market is overbought or oversold. An oscillator becomes overbought, when it reaches a high level associated with market tops occurred in the past. Overbought implies that the price is too high and the market is ready to turn down. An oscillator becomes oversold when it reaches a low level associated with market bottoms occurred in the past. Oversold implies the market is too low and the price is ready to turn up. Overbought and oversold levels are indicated by horizontal reference lines on the charts. However, these levels are somewhat arbitrary and need to be changed from time to time and from market to market.

Secondly, oscillator indicators can be used in the interpretation of divergences, i.e., when they diverge from prices. Bullish divergences occur when prices fall to a new low while an

47

oscillator does not decline to a new low. Bullish divergences quite often spell the end of downtrends. Bearish divergences occur when prices rally to a new high while an oscillator does not rise to a new peak. Bearish divergences quite often spell the ends of up-trends.

An ideal oscillator indicator should lead price by a phase of $\pi/2$ radians, i.e., 90 degrees (see Appendix 4).   However, the conventional oscillator indicators always lag behind this ideal phase. This is probably why it has become necessary to use overbought and oversold levels to signify market turns. The momentum indicator, quite often used by traders, is actually the same as the two point moving difference described in Appendix 4. The moving difference has quite some phase lag from the ideal phase. We will propose two oscillator indicators, the parabolic velocity indicator and the cubic velocity indicator that have very little phase lag from the ideal phase. Velocity measures the rate of change of a quantity with respect to time. At the turning points of the market, the output response of the indicators become zero, thus providing a clear signal for a change in trends. No reference level or any arbitrary parameter is required for their interpretations.   Furthermore, a positive velocity implies that the market is trending up, and a negative velocity implies that the market is trending down. Thus, the velocity indicators can be used as trending indicators as well.

6.1 Parabolic Velocity Indicator

Traders quite often approximate price-time data as piecewise linear and draw straight lines called trendlines through the data. An ascending trendline shows that the market is trending up.   A descending trendline shows that the market is trending down.

However, can price-time data be represented by other curves rather than straight lines? A parabola is the trajectory that a piece of stone will follow when we throw it off the ground. In this case, the parabola curves down. However, the equation of a parabola can be arranged such that it curves up, or curves sideways. Thus, a parabola would seem to be a good candidate to represent market data.   It should particularly be noted that at turning points, it is better to approximate the data as piecewise parabolas than piecewise straight lines. In any case, it can be easily shown in analytical geometry that the equation of a straight line is a particular case of the equation of a parabola. Thus, a parabola would be more versatile than a straight line in representing data. Figure 6.1(a) shows a simulation of market bottom by a parabola concaving up. Figure 6.1(b) shows a straight line which represents the slope or gradient of the parabola (slope is called derivative in Calculus, and can easily be calculated from the equation representing the parabola). The slope is initially negative as the market is going downhill. At the turning point, the slope equals zero. The slope is positive when the market is going uphill.

Figure 6.2(a) shows a simulation of a market top by a parabola concaving down. Figure 6.2(b) shows a straight line which represents the slope or gradient of the parabola. The slope is initially positive as the market is going uphill. At the turning point, the slope equals zero. The slope is negative when the market is going downhill.

All these mean that at market bottom, slope of the price go from negative to positive and is zero at the turning point. At the market top, slope of the price will go from positive to negative and is zero at the turning point. Thus, the slope is an important indicator of market turns. However, given some arbitrary data, how are we going to find the slope? We will introduce here the parabolic velocity indicator, whose derivation will be given in Appendix 4. Basically, three adjacent market price data points are fitted to a parabola. The slope of the parabola at the most recent data point is then calculated using Calculus. The slope would represent the velocity.

The parabolic velocity indicator is defined as (3/2 , −2 , 1/2). Thus, the output response, y, after the input price data, x, is filtered by the indicator is

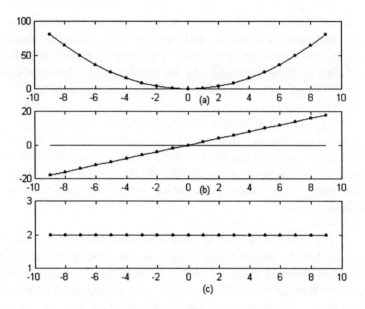

Fig. 6.1. Market price data simulated as a parabola concaving up: (a) the parabola; (b) the slope of the parabola; (c) the slope of the slope of the parabola.

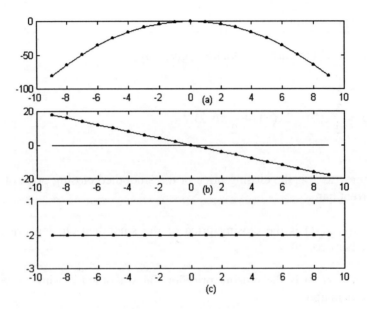

Fig. 6.2. Market price data simulated as a parabola concaving down: (a) the parabola; (b) the slope of the parabola; (c) the slope of the slope of the parabola.

$$y(n) = \frac{3}{2}x(n) - 2x(n-1) + \frac{1}{2}x(n-2) \qquad (6.1)$$

where n is an integer.

Therefore, the current velocity is given by

$$y(0) = \frac{3}{2}x(0) - 2x(-1) + \frac{1}{2}x(-2) \qquad (6.2)$$

where   x(0) is the closing price or the smoothed closing price of the current bar,

x(-1) is the closing price or the smoothed closing price of one bar ago,

x(-2) is the closing price or the smoothed closing price of two bars ago.

Figure 6.3(a) shows a market price data simulated as a sine wave. The slope (or derivative) of the sine wave is plotted in Fig. 6.3(b) and compared with the sine wave filtered by the parabolic velocity indicator. The plot shows that the velocity as calculated yields the slope quite well, thus providing us an easy way to calculate the slope.

In the EasyLanguage code of Omega Research's TradeStation2000i, the program for calculating the parabolic velocity indicator can be written as follows: -

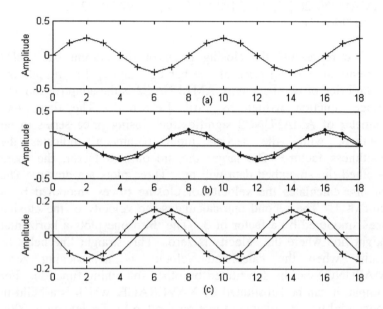

Fig. 6.3. Market price data simulated as a sine wave of circular frequency of π/4 radian: (a) the sine wave; (b) the sine wave filtered by the parabolic velocity indicator (marked as .), and compared with the slope of the sine wave (marked as +); (c) the sine wave filtered by the parabolic acceleration indicator (marked as .), and compared with the slope of the slope of the sine wave (marked as +).

```
Plot1(3*AMAFUNC2(c,1)/2-
2*AMAFUNC2(c[1],1)+AMAFUNC2(c[2],1)/2,"Plot1");
Plot2(3*AMAFUNC2(c,3)/2-
2*AMAFUNC2(c[1],3)+AMAFUNC2(c[2],3)/2,"Plot2");
Plot3(0,"Plot3");
```

c represents the closing price of the current bar. c[1] represents the closing price of one bar ago, and c[2] represents the closing price of two bars ago. AMAFUNC2 is the adaptive moving average function written by Jurik Research. The first input parameter of AMAFUNC2 signifies the closing price series to be smoothed, while the second input parameter indicates the smoothness factor. The larger the smoothness factor, the more smoothed the smoothed data will be. Three plots are drawn. The first one calculates the velocity of closing prices smoothed by a factor of 1. The second one calculates the velocity of the closing prices smoothed by a factor of 3. The third one plots a horizontal straight line where the velocity is zero. This straight line helps to identify when the calculated velocity is approaching zero. AMAFUNC2 can be substituted by other smoothing function. For example, it can be substituted by XAVERAGE, which is a build-in exponential moving average function written by TradeStation2000i. The first input parameter of XAVERAGE signifies the closing price series to be smoothed, while the second input parameter indicates the length of the window (see Chapter 5). The program plotting the parabolic velocity indicators calculated on closing price data smoothed by exponential moving average is listed as follows: -

```
Plot1(3*XAVERAGE(c,3)/2-
2*XAVERAGE(c[1],3)+XAVERAGE(c[2],3)/2,"Plot1");
Plot2(3*XAVERAGE(c,6)/2-
2*XAVERAGE(c[1],6)+XAVERAGE(c[2],6)/2,"Plot2");
Plot3(0,"Plot3");
```

Next we will take a look at the parabolic acceleration indicator to see how the slope of a slope can be simulated.

6.2 Parabolic Acceleration Indicator

Acceleration is the rate of change of velocity. So, if the slope of a curve represents velocity, the slope of the slope of a curve would represent acceleration. The reason that we need to calculate acceleration would be obvious later. Figure 6.1(c) shows the slope of the slope of a concave up parabola (slope of the slope is called second derivative in Calculus, and can easily be calculated from the equation representing the parabola). It is a positive constant. Figure 6.2(c) shows the slope of the slope of a concave down parabola. It is a negative constant. Thus, at market bottom, the slope of the slope is positive. And at market top, the slope of the slope is negative. (It is commonly known in Calculus that when a curve is concaving up, the second derivative is positive; and when the curve is concaving down, the second derivative is negative).

We will define a parabolic acceleration indicator as $(1, -2, 1)$, whose derivation in given in Appendix 4. Basically, three adjacent market price data points are fitted to a parabola. The slope of the slope of the parabola at the most recent data point is then calculated using Calculus. The slope of the slope would represent the acceleration. The output response, y, after the input price data, x, is filtered by the indicator is

$$y(n) = x(n) - 2x(n-1) + x(n-2) \qquad (6.3)$$

Therefore, the current acceleration is given by

$$y(0) = x(0) - 2x(-1) + x(-2) \qquad (6.4)$$

The slope of the slope of the sine wave as calculated from Calculus is plotted in Fig. 6.3(c) and compare with the sine wave filtered by the parabolic acceleration indicator. The plot shows that the acceleration as calculated has a phrase lag from the slope of the slope. This simply means that a sine wave is not very well fitted with piecewise parabolas.

In EasyLanguage code provided by Omega Research's TradeStation2000i, the parabolic acceleration indicator can be written as follows: -

```
Plot1(AMAFUNC2(c,1)-
2*AMAFUNC2(c[1],1)+AMAFUNC2(c[2],1),"Plot1");
Plot2(AMAFUNC2(c,3)-
2*AMAFUNC2(c[1],3)+AMAFUNC2(c[2],3),"Plot2");
Plot3(0,"Plot3");
```

Three plots are drawn. The first one calculates the acceleration of closing prices smoothed by AMAFUNC2 using a smoothness factor of 1. The second one calculates the acceleration of the closing prices smoothed by a factor of 3. The third one plots a horizontal straight line where the acceleration is zero. This straight line helps to identify when the calculated acceleration is approaching zero. AMAFUNC2 can be substituted by XAVERAGE. The program plotting the parabolic acceleration indicators calculated on closing price data smoothed by exponential moving average is listed as follows: -

```
Plot1(XAVERAGE(c,3)-
2*XAVERAGE(c[1],3)+XAVERAGE(c[2],3),"Plot1");
Plot2(XAVERAGE(c,6)-
2*XAVERAGE(c[1],6)+XAVERAGE(c[2],6),"Plot2");
Plot3(0,"Plot3");
```

While the parabolic velocity indicator provides a reasonably good representation of the velocity, the parabolic acceleration indicator has a phase lag compared to the acceleration. We will see in the next section how we can reduce the phase lag using the cubic acceleration indicator. While the parabolic indicators employ only three data points, the cubic indicators will employ four data points.

6.3 Cubic Velocity and Acceleration Indicators

Quite often, market moves in waves and is better approximated by a piecewise cubic function rather than by a piecewise parabola. While a parabola can be considered as a mathematical expression of degree two, a cubic function can be considered as a mathematical expression of degree three. Thus, a cubic function is more versatile than a parabola. In any case, it can be shown in analytical geometry that a parabola is a particular case of a cubic function. Figure 6.4(a) shows a simulation of the market continuation by a single cubic function ($x = n^3$). Figure 6.4(b) shows its slope ($3n^2$, calculated using derivatives in Calculus) which is zero at the turning point (or rather an inflection point). When the market continues in the same direction after the turning point, the slope remains positive. The slope of the slope ($6n$, calculated using derivatives in Calculus) approaches zero near the turning point and points up (Fig. 6.4 (c)). This is quite different from the constant slope of the slope when the market data looks like a parabola (Fig. 6.2(c)). Figure 6.5(a) shows a more complicated cubic function. The data rises to a local maximum, retraces to a local minimum and then continues upwards. (This kind of curve appears in market price data quite often.) Figure 6.5(b) shows its slopes, which are zero at the two turning points, the local maximum and the local minimum. Again, when the market continues in the same original direction after the two turning points, the slope of its slope at the two turning points are close to zero and point up (Fig. 6.5(c)).

Figure 6.6(a) shows a cubic function which falls to a local minimum, retraces to a local maximum and then continues downward. (Again, this kind of curve appears in market price data quite often.) Figure 6.6(b) shows its slopes, which are zero at the two turning points, the local minimum and the local maximum. When the market continues in the same original direction after the two turning points, the slope of its slope at the two turning points are close to zero and point down.

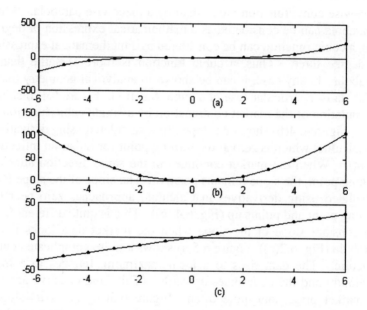

Fig. 6.4. Market price data simulated as a cubic function: (a) the cubic function; (b) the slope of the cubic function; (c) the slope of the slope of the cubic function.

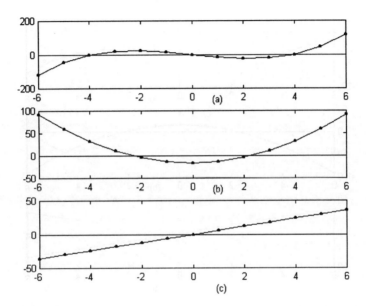

Fig. 6.5. Market price data simulated as a more complicated cubic function continuing in an uptrend: (a) the cubic function; (b) the slope of the cubic function; (c) the slope of the slope of the cubic function.

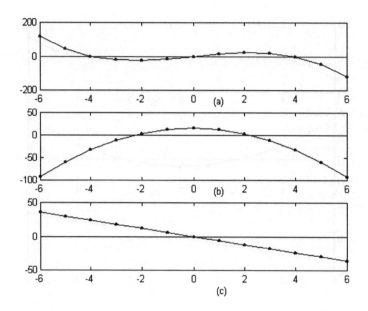

Fig. 6.6. Market price data simulated as a more complicated cubic function continuing in a downtrend: (a) the cubic function; (b) the slope of the cubic function; (c) the slope of the slope of the cubic function.

The slope of the slope is thus significant in differentiating whether the market is experiencing a major turning point or only minor turning points and will continue in the same original direction after. When the market is experiencing a major turning point, the slope of the slope is approximately a constant. When the market is experiencing only a hiccup and will continue in the original direction after, the slope of the slope will point to the direction that it will continue after.

The problem now then is to find a velocity and acceleration indicators to simulate the slope and the slope of the slope respectively with little phase lag (While the parabolic velocity indicator can simulate the slope quite well, the parabolic acceleration indicator has quite a phrase lag from the slope of the slope). The cubic velocity and acceleration indicators will be introduced here and will be used for the rest of the book. Their derivations are given Appendix 4. Basically, four adjacent market price data points are fitted to a cubic function. The slope and the slope of the slope of the cubic function at the most recent data point are then calculated using Calculus. They would represent the velocity and acceleration.

The cubic velocity indicator is defined as (11/6, −3, 3/2, −1/3). The output response, y, after the input price data, x, is filtered by the cubic velocity indicator is

$$y(n) = \frac{11}{6}x(n) - 3x(n-1) + \frac{3}{2}x(n-2) - \frac{1}{3}x(n-3) \qquad (6.5)$$

Therefore, the current velocity is given by

$$y(0) = \frac{11}{6}x(0) - 3x(-1) + \frac{3}{2}x(-2) - \frac{1}{3}x(-3) \qquad (6.6)$$

where   x(0) is the closing price or the smoothed closing price of the current bar

x(−1) is the closing price or the smoothed closing price of one bar ago

x(−2) is the closing price or the smoothed closing price of two bars ago

x(−3) is the closing price or the smoothed closing price of three bars ago

Figure 6.7(a) shows a market price data simulated as a sine wave. The slope of the sine wave, as calculated from Calculus, is plotted in Fig. 6.7(b). The sine wave filtered by the cubic velocity indicator is also plotted, and it agrees quite well with the slope.

In the EasyLanguage code of Omega Research's TradeStation2000i, the program for calculating the cubic velocity indicator can be written as follows: -

```
Plot1(11*AMAFUNC2(c,1)/6-
3*AMAFUNC2(c[1],1)+3*AMAFUNC2(c[2],1)/2-
AMAFUNC2(c[3],1)/3,"Plot1");
Plot2(11*AMAFUNC2(c,3)/6-
3*AMAFUNC2(c[1],3)+3*AMAFUNC2(c[2],3)/2-
AMAFUNC2(c[3],3)/3,"Plot2");
Plot3(0,"Plot3");
```

c represents the closing price of the current bar.   c[1] represents the closing price of one bar ago, c[2] represents the closing price of two bars ago and c[3] represents the closing price of three bars ago.   AMAFUNC2 is the adaptive moving average function written by Jurik Research. Three plots are drawn. The first one calculates the velocity of closing prices smoothed by a factor of 1.   The second one calculates the velocity of the closing prices smoothed by a factor of 3. The third one plots a horizontal straight

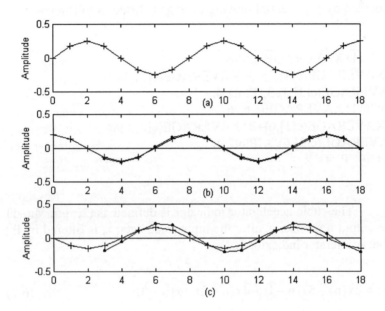

Fig. 6.7. Market price data simulated as a sine wave of circular frequency of π/4 radian: (a) the sine wave; (b) the sine wave filtered by the cubic velocity indicator (marked as .), and compared with the slope of the sine wave (marked as +); (c) the sine wave filtered by the cubic acceleration indicator (marked as .), and compared with the slope of the slope of the sine wave (marked as +).

line where the velocity is zero. This straight line helps to identify when the calculated velocity is approaching zero. AMAFUNC2 can be substituted by other smoothing function. For example, it can be substituted by XAVERAGE, which is a build-in exponential moving average function written by TradeStation2000i. The program plotting the cubic velocity indicators calculated on closing price data smoothed by exponential moving average is listed as follows: -

```
Plot1(11*XAVERAGE(c,3)/6-
3*XAVERAGE(c[1],3)+3*XAVERAGE(c[2],3)/2-
XAVERAGE(c[3],3)/3,"Plot1");
Plot2(11*XAVERAGE(c,6)/6-
3*XAVERAGE(c[1],6)+3*XAVERAGE(c[2],6)/2-
XAVERAGE(c[3],6)/3,"Plot2");
Plot3(0,"Plot3");
```

The cubic accelerator indicator is defined as $(2, -5, 4, -1)$. The output response, y, after the input price data, x, is filtered by the cubic accelerator indicator is

$$y(n) = 2x(n) - 5x(n-1) + 4x(n-2) - x(n-3) \qquad (6.7)$$

Therefore, the current acceleration is given by

$$y(0) = 2x(0) - 5x(-1) + 4x(-2) - x(-3) \qquad (6.8)$$

It should be noted that parabolic as well as cubic velocity and acceleration indicators are examples of convolution sums as depicted in Eq (4.3).

Figure 6.7(c) plots the slope of the slope of the sine wave as calculated from Calculus. The sine wave filtered by the cubic acceleration indicator is also plotted and it agrees reasonably well with the slope of the slope. It has a much less phase lag compared with the sine wave filtered by the parabolic acceleration indicator (Fig. 6.3(c)). The agreement would be even much better if the sine wave is sampled more frequently (Fig. 6.8).

Figure 6.9(a) shows a market price data simulated as a summation of two sine waves. Its slope (calculated by using Calculus) is plotted in Fig. 6.9(b) and it agrees quite well with the sine waves filtered by the cubic velocity indicator. Figure 6.9(c) plots the slope of the slope (calculated by using Calculus). It agrees reasonably well with the sine waves filtered by the cubic acceleration indicator. At sample number 34, the market price is experiencing a minor turning point. While the velocity is approximately zero, the acceleration is slightly less than zero and pointing toward the direction where the market will continue. The acceleration implies that the curve may change from concave down to concave up, and the market will go up after a slow down. In a slightly different perspective, since acceleration represents the slope of the velocity, the acceleration here implies that the velocity may change its slope from negative to positive, generating the expectation that the velocity will remain positive and the market will go up. This scenario can be contrasted with sample number 8, which is a major turning point. While the velocity is zero, the acceleration is negative, implying that the market is concaving down. The acceleration is also pointing in the direction where the market is heading. This can be compared with Fig. 6.2 when a major turning point is simulated as a parabola. While the velocity is zero at the turning point, the acceleration is a constant and far from zero.

In the EasyLanguage code of Omega Research's TradeStation2000i, the program for calculating the cubic acceleration indicator can be written as follows: -

```
Plot1(2*AMAFUNC2(c,1)-
5*AMAFUNC2(c[1],1)+4*AMAFUNC2(c[2],1)-
AMAFUNC2(c[3],1),"Plot1");
```

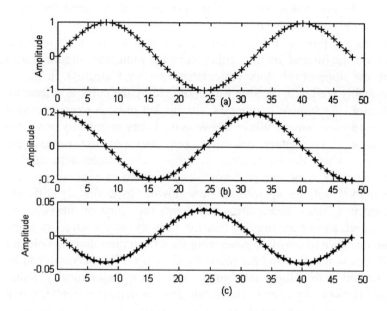

Fig. 6.8. Market price data simulated as a sine wave of circular frequency of $\pi/16$ radian: (a) the sine wave; (b) the sine wave filtered by the cubic velocity indicator (marked as .), and compared with the slope of the sine wave (marked as +); (c) the sine wave filtered by the cubic acceleration indicator (marked as .), and compared with the slope of the slope of the sine wave (marked as +).

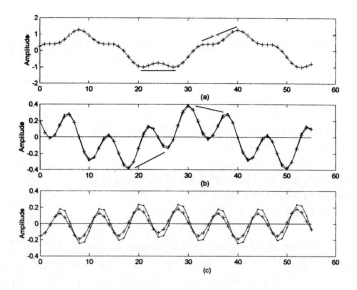

Fig. 6.9. Market price data simulated as a summation of sine waves of circular frequency of $\pi/16$ radian with amplitude 1.0 and $\pi/4$ radian with amplitude 0.25, showing double bottoms: (a) the summation of sine waves; (b) the summation of sine waves filtered by the cubic velocity indicator (marked as .), and compared with the slope of the summation of sine waves (marked as +); (c) the summation of sine waves filtered by the cubic acceleration indicator (marked as .), and compared with the slope of the slope of the summation of sine waves (marked as +). Class A bearish and Class B bullish divergences are illustrated here.

Plot2(2*AMAFUNC2(c,3)-
5*AMAFUNC2(c[1],3)+4*AMAFUNC2(c[2],3)-
AMAFUNC2(c[3],3),"Plot2");
Plot3(0,"Plot3");

AMAFUNC2 is the adaptive moving average function. Other smoothing functions can replace this function. The program plotting the cubic acceleration indicators calculated on closing price data smoothed by exponential moving average is listed as follows: -

Plot1(2*XAVERAGE(c,3)-
5*XAVERAGE(c[1],3)+4*XAVERAGE(c[2],3)-
XAVERAGE(c[3],3),"Plot1");
Plot2(2*XAVERAGE(c,6)-
5*XAVERAGE(c[1],6)+4*XAVERAGE(c[2],6)-
XAVERAGE(c[3],6),"Plot2");
Plot3(0,"Plot3");

Figure 6.10 shows a 15-minute chart of the US 30 year Treasury Bond Future. The price data was smoothed using the adaptive moving average with smoothness 1 (thin line) and smoothness 3 (thick line). Cubic velocity indicators were applied to the moving averages and plotted in the middle of the figure. Cubic acceleration indicators were also applied to the moving averages and plotted in the bottom of the figure. At 11:50 am, the market as shown by the adaptive moving average with a smoothness factor of 3 (ama3) continued to trend down. However, the velocity, as represented by the cubic velocity indicator of ama3 (thick line), approached zero from a negative value in a somewhat linear fashion. The acceleration, as represented by the cubic acceleration indicator of ama3 (thick line) is away from zero and approximately a positive constant, thus implying that the curvature of ama3 of the price data is concaving up. This can be compared with the parabola, its slope and the slope of its slope in Fig. 6.1. The velocity and acceleration in Fig. 6.10 indicated that a major turning point is imminent. After the turning point, the velocity of ama3 remains positive for the whole

Fig. 6.10. A 15-minute chart of an US 30 year Treasury Bond Future, showing a turning point at the market bottom. Cubic velocity and cubic acceleration indicators are plotted in the middle and bottom figures respectively. *Chart produced with Omega Research TradeStation2000i.*

afternoon, implying that the slope of the curve is positive and the market is trending up. A day-trader who has bought at the turning point can hold the contract until the end of the day.

Figure 6.11 shows another 15-minute chart of the US 30 years Treasury Bond Future. The price data was again smoothed using the adaptive moving average with smoothness 1 (thin line) and smoothness 3 (thick line). The Bond trended up in the morning. At 12:05 p.m., it appeared as if it was running out of steam and will turn down. However, the velocity of ama3 approached zero in a parabolic fashion. Furthermore, the acceleration of ama3 approached zero from a negative value in an approximately linear fashion. These indications implied that the market might continue upwards. This phenomenon is very similar to the cubic function, its slope, and the slope of its slope in Fig. 6.5. As it happened, the market did continue upwards in the afternoon.

A word of caution needs to be emphasized. As described in Chapter 3, a model can never be perfect in describing real phenomenon. When market price data points are fitted to a cubic function, we are modeling market behavior as piecewise cubic and expect it to behave as such in the very near future. This, of course, does not have to be the case, as the market can do whatever it wants to do.

Nevertheless, the cubic velocity and acceleration indicators are better oscillator tools to increase the probability of forecasting when turning points in the market would occur. In addition, they can be used to explain some of the common market phenomena like divergences and head and shoulders:

6.4 Divergences

Books on technical analysis quite often discuss about divergences, i.e. when oscillators diverge from prices. Divergences can give

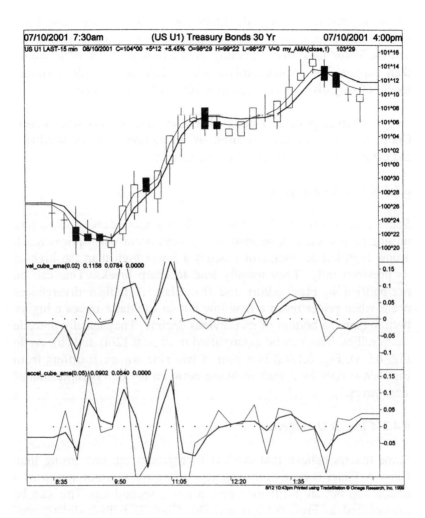

Fig. 6.11.   A 15-minute chart of an US 30 year Treasury Bond Future, showing a continuation pattern. Cubic velocity and cubic acceleration indicators are plotted in the middle and bottom figures respectively. *Chart produced with Omega Research TradeStation2000i.*

out some good trading signals (Elder 1993). Divergences have been divided into three classes, depending upon how the patterns of price and oscillator look like. Trading books only tell you what would then happen, but do not explain why. Here we provide a simple model of why divergences lead to turnings of market trends.

Market price is simulated as the sum of two sine waves. Cubic velocity indicator is used as an example of an oscillator indicator. The three classes of divergences are:

6.4.1 *Class A Divergence*

Some traders believe that class A divergences identify important turning points. Class A bearish divergences occur when prices reach a new high but an oscillator reaches a lower high than the high of its previous rally. They usually lead to sharp breaks. This can be exemplified in Figs. 6.9(a) and (b). Class A bullish divergences occur when prices reach a new low but an oscillator traces a higher bottom than the bottom of its previous decline. They usually precede sharp rallies. This can be exemplified in Figs. 6.12(a) and (b). As in Fig. 6.9(a), Fig. 6.12(a) is a sum of two sine waves. It differs from Fig. 6.9(a) only by a shift in phase between the two components of sine waves.

6.4.2 *Class B Divergence*

Some traders believe that class B divergences are less strong than Class A. Class B bearish divergences occur when prices appear as a double top but an oscillator traces a lower second top. This can be exemplified in Figs. 6.12(a) and (b). Class B bullish divergences occur when prices appear as a double bottom but an oscillator traces a higher second bottom. This can be exemplified in Figs. 6.9(a) and (b).

6.4.3 *Class C Divergence*

Some traders believe that class C divergences are the least

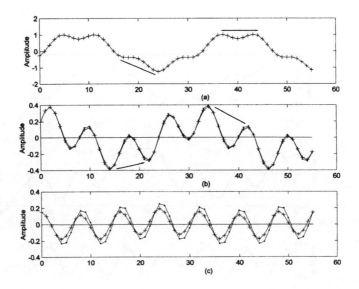

Fig. 6.12. Market price data simulated as a summation of sine waves of circular frequency of π/16 radian with amplitude 1.0 and π/4 radian with amplitude 0.25, showing double tops: (a) the summation of sine waves; (b) the summation of sine waves filtered by the cubic velocity indicator (marked as .), and compared with the slope of the summation of sine waves (marked as +); (c) the summation of sine waves filtered by the cubic acceleration indicator (marked as .), and compared with the slope of the slope of the summation of sine waves (marked as +). Class A bullish and Class B bearish divergences are illustrated here.

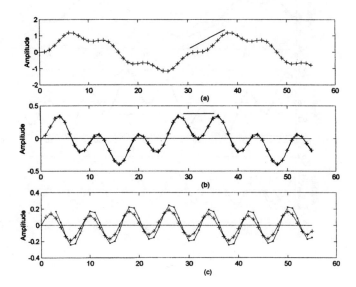

Fig. 6.13. Market price data simulated as a summation of sine waves of circular frequency of π/16 radian with amplitude 1.0 and π/4 radian with amplitude 0.25: (a) the summation of sine waves; (b) the summation of sine waves filtered by the cubic velocity indicator (marked as .), and compared with the slope of the summation of sine waves (marked as +); (c) the summation of sine waves filtered by the cubic acceleration indicator (marked as .), and compared with the slope of the slope of the summation of sine waves (marked as +). Class C bearish divergence is illustrated here.

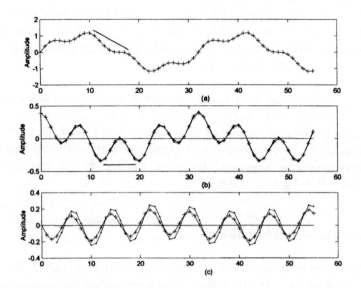

Fig. 6.14. Market price data simulated as a summation of sine waves of circular frequency of π/16 radian with amplitude 1.0 and π/4 radian with amplitude 0.25: (a) the summation of sine waves; (b) the summation of sine waves filtered by the cubic velocity indicator (marked as .), and compared with the slope of the summation of sine waves (marked as +); (c) the summation of sine waves filtered by the cubic acceleration indicator (marked as .), and compared with the slope of the slope of the summation of sine waves (marked as +). Class C bullish divergence is illustrated here.

important. Class C bearish divergences occur when prices rise to a new high but the oscillator forms a double top. This can be exemplified in Figs. 6.13(a) and (b). As in Fig. 6.9(a), Fig. 6.13(a) is a sum of two sine waves. It differs from Fig. 6.9(a) only by a shift in phase between the two components of sine waves. Class C bullish divergences occur when prices fall to a new low but the oscillator traces a double bottom. This can be exemplified in Figs. 6.14(a) and (b). As in Fig. 6.9(a), Fig. 6.14(a) is a sum of two sine waves. Again, it differs from Fig. 6.9(a) only by a shift in phase between the two components of sine waves.

Our model of simulating price as the summation of two sine waves with varying relative phrases between them thus easily explain all classes of divergences. Our model does not really display the varying degrees of significance for different classes of divergences as suggested by some traders, as we can see from Figs. 6.9, 6.12, 6.13 and 6.14.

6.5 Head and Shoulders

This pattern consists of a final rally, which is called the head, separating two smaller rallies, which are called the shoulders. This is a reversal pattern, signifying that the bulls are losing their grip. An uptrend fails to reach a higher high, and a decline falls below the previous low. Our model of the summation of two sine waves can simulate the head and shoulders tops quite well (Fig. 6.15(a)). Figure 6.15(a) differs from Fig. 6.9(a) by a change in amplitude between the two components of sine waves. Figure 6.15(b) shows that the oscillator tops declines, illustrating that the uptrend is over.

An inverse head and shoulders is the opposite of head and shoulders. It signifies that the downtrend is over. Figure 6.16(a) shows a summation of two sine waves simulating an inverse head and shoulders pattern. Figure 6.16(a) differs from Fig. 6.15(a) only by a shift in phase between the two components of sine waves. The corresponding oscillator bottoms in Fig. 6.16(b) increases, showing that the bulls are gaining ground.

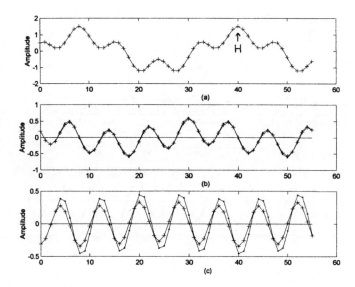

Fig. 6.15. Market price data simulated as a summation of sine waves of circular frequency of $\pi/16$ radians with amplitude 1.0 and $\pi/4$ radian with amplitude 0.5: (a) the summation of sine waves. The pattern looks like head (denoted as H) and shoulders; (b) the summation of sine waves filtered by the cubic velocity indicator (marked as .), and compared with the slope of the summation of sine waves (marked as +); (c) the summation of sine waves filtered by the cubic acceleration indicator (marked as .), and compared with the slope of the slope of the summation of sine waves (marked as +).

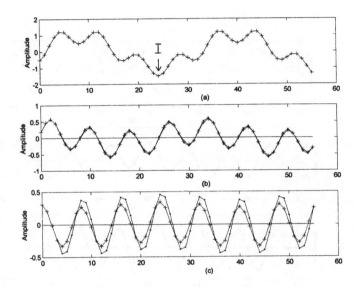

Fig. 6.16. Market price data simulated as a summation of sine waves of circular frequency of $\pi/16$ radians with amplitude 1.0 and $\pi/4$ radian with amplitude 0.5: (a) the summation of sine waves. The pattern looks like inverse head (denoted as I) and shoulders; (b) the summation of sine waves filtered by the cubic velocity indicator (marked as .), and compared with the slope of the summation of sine waves (marked as +); (c) the summation of sine waves filtered by the cubic acceleration indicator (marked as .), and compared with the slope of the slope of the summation of sine waves (marked as +).

Chapter 7

Vertex Indicators

The velocity indicators introduced in the last chapter help to determine the turning points of the market trends. However, in a slow market, the trend sometimes turns slowly, and it takes a long time for the velocity (or slope) of the price data to approach zero, which corresponds to the turning point. To help determine more accurately when exactly the market is going to turn, two new indicators, the parabolic vertex and the cubic vertex indicators are introduced. Vertex in a curve is the point where the slope of the curve changes direction, i.e., from positive to negative, or vice-versa. In other words, the vertex is the turning point. The vertex indicators will show what time the market has turned, or, more importantly, what time in the future the market will turn.

7.1 Parabolic Vertex Indicator

Market price is simulated as a parabola. More specially, three adjacent market price data points are fitted to a parabola. The parabolic vertex indicator calculates $t_v(n)$, the number of bars the turning point is from the nth bar (the symbol t represents time). A bar is a time unit, which can be chosen to be a week, a day, 60 minutes, etc. For example, if the vertex indicator yields a number of +3, it means that it is forecasted that the market will turn 3 bars ahead of the nth bar. If n is chosen to be zero, and a bar is taken to be a day, it would simply mean that the market will turn 3 days from now. Similarly, −2 means that the market has turned 2 bars ago from the

79

n^{th} bar. Again, if n is chosen to be zero, and a bar is taken to be a day, it would mean that the market has already turned two days ago. $t_v(n)$ is given by

$$t_v(n) = \frac{-\left[\dfrac{3}{2}x(n) - 2x(n-1) + \dfrac{1}{2}x(n-2)\right]}{x(n) - 2x(n-1) + x(n-2)} \tag{7.1}$$

where x is the closing price or the smoothed closing prices. The derivation of Eq (7.1) is shown in Appendix 5. If the denominator of Eq (7.1) is zero, it means that the data lie on a straight line and no turning point exists. A very large arbitrary number is assigned to $t_v(n)$ in the computer program to indicate that no vertex is found. When $t_v(n)$ is plotted in a narrow range in a chart, the large number will not be plotted. To calculate the number of bars the vertex or turning point is from the present time, where n = 0,

$$t_v(0) = \frac{-\left[\dfrac{3}{2}x(0) - 2x(-1) + \dfrac{1}{2}x(-2)\right]}{x(0) - 2x(-1) + x(-2)} \tag{7.2}$$

where   x(0) is the closing price or the smoothed closing price of the current bar

x(−1) is the closing price or the smoothed closing price of one bar ago

x(−2) is the closing price or the smoothed closing price of two bars ago

Figure 7.1(a) shows market price being simulated as a parabola and Fig. 7.1(b) shows its slope. Figure 7.1(c) shows the number of bars from the vertex of the parabola, which is located for convenience at sample number = 0. At the vertex, the number of bars from the vertex is zero, which obviously should be the case. The slope at the vertex is also zero at that point. Thus, the parabolic vertex indicator confirms with the slope to locate where the vertex is. In addition, it will forecast when it is going to happen. For example, when the number of bars from vertex is +2, this indicates that the vertex will occur 2 bars from that time. The identification of timing of the vertex is particularly useful when the market is slow and the slope of the market price approaches zero slowly. This can be exemplified in Figs. 7.2(a) and (b). The curvature of the parabola in Fig. 7.2(a) is much smaller than the curvature of the parabola in Fig. 7.1(a), and its slope, as shown in Fig. 7.2(b) is not as steep as that shown in Fig. 7.1(b), thus making it difficult to identify when the market is going to turn. However, since the parabolic vertex indicator is not affected by the slowness of the market, it can provide a much clearer picture of when the turning point will happen, as shown in Fig. 7.2(c).

7.2 Cubic Vertex Indicator

As discussed in the last chapter, market price data are quite often better approximated by a cubic function. In any case, a parabola is a special case of a cubic function. A cubic vertex indicator can yield two vertices or turning points, as a cubic function usually have two turning points. $t_\pm(n)$, the number of bars the turning points are from the nth bar, are given by

$$t_\pm(n) = \frac{-d \pm \sqrt{d^2 - 3ce}}{3c} \tag{7.3}$$

where $c = [x(n) - 3x(n-1) + 3x(n-2) - x(n-3)]/6 \neq 0$ (7.4)

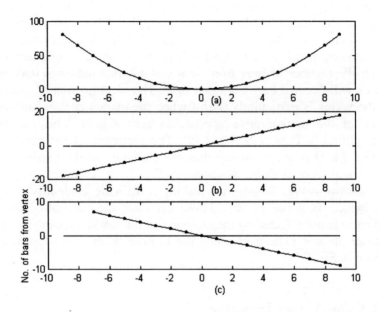

Fig. 7.1. Market price data simulated as a parabola concaving up: (a) the parabola; (b) the slope of the parabola; (c) number of bars from vertex (or turning point) of the parabola, as calculated from the parabolic vertex indicator. Numbers on the horizontal axis are sample numbers.

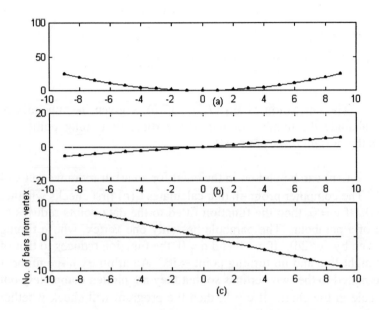

Fig. 7.2. Market price data simulated as a parabola concaving up, the parabola has a smaller concavity than that of Fig. 7.1: (a) the parabola; (b) the slope of the parabola; (c) number of bars from vertex (or turning point) of the parabola, as calculated from the parabolic vertex indicator.

$$d = [2x(n)-5x(n-1)+4x(n-2)-x(n-3)]/2 \qquad (7.5)$$

$$e = [11x(n)-18x(n-1)+9x(n-2)-2x(n-3)]/6 \qquad (7.6)$$

and x is the closing or the smoothed closing price.

The derivation of Eq (7.3) – (7.6) is given in Appendix 5. To calculate the number of bars the vertices or turning points are from the present time, put n = 0.

$t_{\pm}(n)$ can be plotted in the chart for an arbitrary range, e.g., -4 to 4. The computer program that calculates $t_{\pm}(n)$ first checks whether c = 0. If c = 0, then the function fitted to the data points reduces to that of a parabola. The parabola has only one vertex, whose timing is given by $-e/(2d)$. If c = 0 and d = 0, the function reduces to that of a straight line and no turning point exits. An arbitrary large number is assigned to the two vertices so that they are plotted completely out of scale in the chart. If c ≠ 0, then the program will check whether (a) $(d^2-3ce) < 0$ (b) $(d^2-3ce) = 0$ (c) $(d^2-3ce) > 0$.

For case (a), no vertex exists, an arbitrary large number is assigned to each of the two vertices so that they are plotted completely out of scale in the chart. For case (b), the two vertices are actually the same vertex, $t_+ = t_- = -d/(3c)$. For case (c), the values of the two vertices are compared, the larger one is assigned to t_2 and the smaller one to t_1 . t_2 is the timing of the turning point which is closer to the present time. t_2 will usually show what will happen in the future and t_1 usually shows what has happened in the past. The computer program can choose to plot t_2 only as the future is generally what traders are interested in.

Figure 7.3(a) shows some market price data simulated by a cubic function, and Fig. 7.3(b) shows its slope. The two vertices of the cubic function have slopes equal to zero. Figure 7.3(c) shows the number of bars from a vertex at a certain time (or a certain sample number). This is calculated from the cubic vertex indicator. The position of the first vertex (which takes on the negative sign of Eq (7.3) in this example), is, by definition, smaller than that of the second vertex (which takes on the positive sign of Eq (7.3) in this example). The cubic vertex indicator identifies the past as well as forecast the future vertex very well.

Figure 7.4(a) shows a sine wave with 12 samples/cycle. Fig. 7.4(b) shows the sine wave being filtered by the cubic velocity indicator, which agree almost exactly with the slope of the sine wave. Figure 7.4(c) shows the number of bars from the vertices of the sine wave as calculated by the cubic vertex operator. The position of the first vertex describes what happened in the past. The position of the second vertex mostly describes what will happen in the future. Table 7.1 compares the estimated number of bars (calculated from the vertex indicator) with the theoretical one. Sample number 5 to 10 are chosen arbitrarily from Fig. 7.4 and are representative of the whole sine wave, which is periodic. Except for sample number 10, the estimated number of bars from the first vertex agrees with the theoretical ones quite well. It should be noted that the cubic vertex operator used only four data points (samples) to explain the past, as well as forecast the future at the same time. The inaccuracy at sample number 10 is simply because the data points are too far away from the vertex. The estimated number of bars from the second vertex attempts to forecast how many bars ahead will there be a turning point. At sample number 5, the estimated number of bars ahead is 13 while the actual number is 4. While this is far from accurate, it does tell you to anticipate a turning point ahead. As the data points get closer and closer to the turning point, the forecast gets more and more accurate until the estimated value agrees exactly with the theoretical value of zero at the turning point.

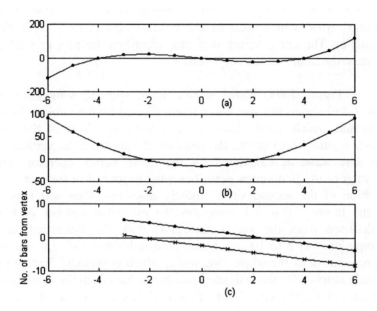

Fig. 7.3. Market price data simulated as a cubic function: (a) the cubic function; (b) the slope of the cubic function; (c) the number of bars from the first (marked as x) and second vertex (marked as .) of the cubic function, as calculated from the cubic vertex indicator.

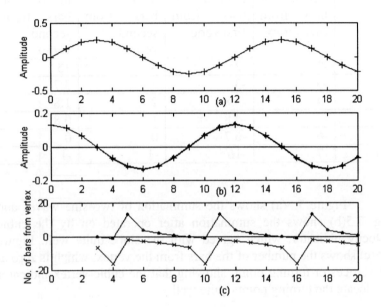

Fig. 7.4. Market price data simulated as a sine wave of circular frequency of π/6 radian: (a) the sine wave; (b) the sine wave filtered by the cubic velocity indicator (marked as .), and compared with the slope of the sine wave (marked as +); (c) the number of bars from the first (marked as x) and second vertex (marked as .) of the sine wave, as calculated from the cubic vertex indicator. Numbers on the horizontal axis are sample numbers.

Table 7.1

Sample Number	Theoretical number of bars from first vertex	Estimated number of bars from first vertex	Theoretical number of bars from second vertex	Estimated number of bars from second vertex
5	-2	-2	4	13
6	-3	-3	3	3.7
7	-4	-3.8	2	1.8
8	-5	-4.8	1	0.8
9	-6	-6.7	0	0
10	-7	-16	-1	-1

Figure 7.5(a) shows the summation of two sine waves and Fig. 7.5(b) shows the summation after operated on by the cubic velocity indicator, which agreed with the slope quite well. Figure 7.5(c) shows the number of the bars from the vertex, which is zero at all vertices or turning point, showing that the cubic vertex indicator can locate the turning points quite well.

In the EasyLanguage code of Omega Research's TradeStation2000i, the program for calculating the closest turning point (i.e, the second vertex t_2) can be written as follows: -

{Program to calculate the time when the closest turning point has occurred or will occur. Closing prices are smoothed by ama1 or ama3}

Variables:
c1(0),d1(0),e1(0),xama1_1(0),xama1_2(0),xama1_p(0),xama1_n(0),
dsq1(0),c3(0),d3(0),e3(0),xama3_1(0),xama3_2(0),xama3_p(0),xam
a3_n(0),dsq3(0);
{Closing prices are smoothed with adaptive moving average with a smoothness factor of 1, ama1}

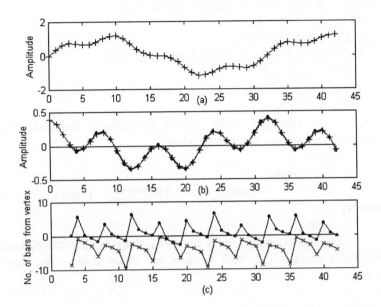

Fig. 7.5. Market price data simulated as a summation of sine waves of circular frequency of $\pi/16$ radian with amplitude 1.0 and $\pi/4$ radian with amplitude 0.25: (a) the summation of sine waves; (b) the summation of sine waves filtered by the cubic velocity indicator (marked as .), and compared with the slope of the summation of sine waves (marked as +); (c) the number of bars from the first (marked as x) and second vertex (marked as .) of the summation of sine waves, as calculated from the cubic vertex indicator.

c1=(AMAFUNC2(c,1)-
3*AMAFUNC2(c[1],1)+3*AMAFUNC2(c[2],1)-
AMAFUNC2(c[3],1))/6;
d1=(2*AMAFUNC2(c,1)-
5*AMAFUNC2(c[1],1)+4*AMAFUNC2(c[2],1)-
AMAFUNC2(c[3],1))/2;
e1=11*AMAFUNC2(c,1)/6-
3*AMAFUNC2(c[1],1)+3*AMAFUNC2(c[2],1)/2-
AMAFUNC2(c[3],1)/3;
If c1=0 Then Begin {cubic function is reduced to a parabola}
      If d1 = 0 Then
            xamal_1 = 99 {cubic function is reduced to a
straight line, which has no turning point}
        Else
        Begin
            xamal_1= −e1/(2*d1); {vertex of a
parabola}
      end;
      xamal_2=xamal_1; {for parabola, there is only one turning
point; for a straight line, both vertices are assigned to a very large
number}
end;
dsq1=Square(d1)−3*c1*e1;
If c1<>0 Then Begin
      If dsq1 < 0 Then Begin {value inside the square root sign is
negative, there is no solution}
          If xamal_1>0 Then   xamal_1 = 99 {If previous
turning point is positive, the current turning point would be assigned
to a very large positive number}
        Else
            xamal_1 = −99 ; {If previous turning point
is negative, the current turning point would be assigned to a very
large negative number}
        If xamal_2>0 Then xamal_2= 99 {If previous
turning point is positive, the current turning point would be assigned
to a very large positive number}
        Else

xama1_2 = −99 ; {If previous turning point is negative, the current turning point would be assigned to a very large negative number}
  end;
  If dsq1 = 0 Then Begin {value inside the square root sign is zero, there is only one solution}
    xama1_1 = −d1/(3*c1) ;
      xama1_2 = xama1_1;
  end;
  If dsq1 > 0 Then Begin {value inside the square root sign is positive, there are two solutions}
    xama1_p = (-d1+Squareroot(dsq1))/(3*c1) ;
      xama1_n= (-d1-Squareroot(dsq1))/(3*c1);
      If xama1_p > xama1_n Then Begin
      xama1_1 = xama1_n;
      xama1_2= xama1_p; {second vertex is the vertex which is closer to the current time}
      end;
      If xama1_n > xama1_p Then Begin
      xama1_1 = xama1_p;
      xama1_2 = xama1_n; {second vertex is the vertex which is closer to the current time}
      end;
    end;
end;
{Closing prices are smoothed with adaptive moving average with a smoothness factor of 3, ama3}
c3=(AMAFUNC2(c,3)-
3*AMAFUNC2(c[1],3)+3*AMAFUNC2(c[2],3)-
AMAFUNC2(c[3],3))/6;
d3=(2*AMAFUNC2(c,3)-
5*AMAFUNC2(c[1],3)+4*AMAFUNC2(c[2],3)-
AMAFUNC2(c[3],3))/2;
e3=11*AMAFUNC2(c,3)/6-
3*AMAFUNC2(c[1],3)+3*AMAFUNC2(c[2],3)/2-
AMAFUNC2(c[3],3)/3;
If c3=0 Then Begin {cubic function is reduced to a parabola}
  If d3 = 0 Then

xama3_1 = 99 {cubic function is reduced to a straight line, which has no turning point}
        Else
            Begin
                    xama3_1= $-e3/(2*d3)$; {vertex of a parabola}
          end;
        xama3_2=xama3_1; {for parabola, there is only one turning point; for a straight line, both vertices are assigned to a very large number}
end;
dsq3=Square(d3)-3*c3*e3;
If c3<>0 Then Begin
        If dsq3 < 0 Then Begin {value inside the square root sign is negative, there is no solution}
               If xama3_1>0 Then   xama3_1 = 99 {If previous turning point is positive, the current turning point would be assigned to a very large positive number}
               Else
                    xama3_1 = -99 ; {If previous turning point is negative, the current turning point would be assigned to a very large negative number}
               If xama3_2>0 Then xama3_2= 99 {If previous turning point is positive, the current turning point would be assigned to a very large positive number}
               Else
                    xama3_2 = -99 ; {If previous turning point is negative, the current turning point would be assigned to a very large negative number}
        end;
        If dsq3 = 0 Then Begin {value inside the square root sign is zero, there is only one solution}
            xama3_1 = -d3/(3*c3) ;
                xama3_2 = xama3_1;
        end;
        If dsq3 > 0 Then Begin {value inside the square root sign is positive, there are two solutions}
            xama3_p = (-d3+Squareroot(dsq3))/(3*c3) ;

```
        xama3_n = (-d3-Squareroot(dsq3))/(3*c3);
              If xama3_p > xama3_n Then Begin
              xama3_1 = xama3_n;
              xama3_2 = xama3_p; {second vertex is the vertex
which is closer to the current time}
              end;
              If xama3_n > xama3_p Then Begin
              xama3_1 = xama3_p;
              xama3_2 = xama3_n; {second vertex is the vertex
which is closer to the current time}
              end;
        end;
end;
Plot1(xama1_2,"Plot1");
Plot2(xama3_2,"Plot2");
Plot3(0,"Plot3");
```

In the above program, AMAFUNC2 is an adaptive moving average function written by Jurik Research. The closing price data is first smoothed with AMAFUNC2 of smoothness factor 1 and 3. These functions can be replaced by other smoothing functions, e.g., XAVERAGE of window length of 3 and 6. XAVERAGE is an exponential moving average function provided by TradeStation2000i.

Figure 7.6 shows a 15-minute chart of the U.S. 30 year Treasury Bond Future. The price is filtered by the adaptive moving average with smoothness of 1 (thin line) and 3 (thick line). After dropping for the whole morning, the market turns up at 11:50 a.m. The velocity of ama3 (shown as the thick line in the second plot), as calculated from the cubic velocity indicator, approaches zero from a negative value. (The thin line corresponds to the velocity of ama1). The acceleration of ama3 (shown as the thick line in the third plot), as calculated from the cubic acceleration indicator, is approximately constant indicating that it is a major turning point. (The thin line

Fig. 7.6. A 15-minute chart of an US 30 year Treasury Bond Future, showing a turning point at the market bottom. Cubic velocity and cubic acceleration indicators are plotted in the second and third figures respectively. The number of bars from the second vertex (or turning point), as calculated from the cubic vertex indicator, is plotted in the bottom figure. *Chart produced with Omega Research TradeStation2000i.*

corresponds to the acceleration of ama1). Only the number of bars from the larger vertex (or second vertex) is plotted in the bottom plot as it usually represents future turning points. The thick line and the thin line represent the cubic vertex indicator operated on the price after it has been smoothed by ama3 and ama1 respectively. Only the number of bars that lie within −4 and +4 are plotted as only values which are close to zero show higher accuracy. At 11:35 a.m., the number of bars from the larger vertex, as calculated from the Bond price smoothed by ama3 is approximately equal to one, implying that the market will turn 1 bar (15 minutes) later. At 11:50 a.m., the number of bars approaches zero (marked by an arrow) and crosses zero after. For the whole afternoon, it remains above zero, which is consistent with the market slowly trending up after the turning point. Some of the vertex points have been assigned an arbitrary very large number, which are shown as almost vertical straight lines in the plot. These would mean that the market price data either fit into a straight line (which has no turning point) or a cubic function that has no turning point. These can imply that the market is not going to turn any sooner (A particular case is that market price data is almost horizontal).

Figure 7.7 shows another 15-minute chart of US 30 year Treasury Bond. The price is filtered by the adaptive moving average (ama) with smoothness of 1 (thin line) and 3 (thick line). The market rises in the morning and then hesitates before noon. It then turns back up at 12:35 p.m (marked by the first arrow in the bottom plot). The number of bars from the larger vertex (shown as the thick line in the bottom plot), as calculated from the Bond price smoothed by ama3 is zero, indicating a turning point exists at that time. This is confirmed by the velocity of ama3, as calculated from the cubic velocity indicator (shown as the thick line in the second plot), being zero. (The thin line corresponds to the velocity of ama1). As the market is turning very slowly, the cubic vertex indicator provides a more accurate timing of the turning point than the cubic velocity

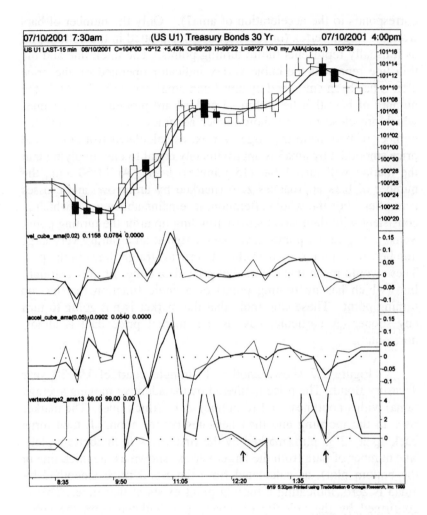

Fig. 7.7. A 15-minute chart of an US 30 year Treasury Bond Future, showing a continuation pattern. Cubic velocity and cubic acceleration indicators are plotted in the second and third plots respectively. The number of bars from the second vertex (or turning point), as calculated from the cubic vertex indicator, is plotted in the bottom plot. *Chart produced with Omega Research TradeStation2000i.*

indicator in this case. As well, it is able to forecast the turning point 2 bars (30 minutes) ahead. At 12:35 pm, the slightly positive acceleration of ama3, as calculated from the cubic acceleration indicator (shown as the thick line in the third plot), shows that the curve is concaving up, illustrating that the market will continue trending up. (The thin line corresponds to the acceleration of ama1). At 2:05 p.m.(marked by the second arrow in the bottom plot), the number of bars from the larger vertex, as calculated from the Bond price smoothed by ama3 is again zero, indicating another turning point. This, again, is consistent with the velocity being zero at that point. The acceleration is negative, implying that the market is going to fall. The market did fall after. In the vertex plot (bottom plot), some of the vertex points have been assigned arbitrary large numbers, implying that the market is not going to turn soon.

The cubic vertex indicator thus can locate turning points quite well. It can be used to confirm the results of the cubic velocity indicator. Furthermore, when the market is turning slowly, the cubic vertex indicator will more clearly identify when the market is going to turn. It can also pinpoint the turning point 1 or 2 bars ahead of time. When the market price data can be fitted to a straight line or a cubic function that has no turning point, this can imply that a turning point is not to be foreseen in the near future.

A word of caution is in order. We are modeling market price data as a piecewise cubic function. The market, of course, does not have to behave as such. However, a piecewise cubic function provides a more versatile tool than a piecewise straight line, which is used by some of the traders. And, as discussed earlier, a straight line can be considered as a particular case of a cubic function. The cubic function would automatically reduce to a straight line when the price data is best fitted to a straight line. As such, the cubic function provides an advantage in trading.

Chapter 8

Various Timeframes

Traders quite often look at charts of different time frames at the same time. They may use a long-term time chart to decide on the set of conditions that are necessary for taking a position in the market. Then they would wait for an indication in a short-term time chart before entering a market (Elder 1993). But why would traders bother to look at different charts? Before we delve into this question, let us take a look at how time charts are made of.

In each time chart, the data are taken from a raw signal by sampling at equal time intervals. The raw price signal in the financial market is the tick data. A tick is an upward or downward price movement. In a 15-minute chart, the data is sampled at a 15 minute interval, i.e., the closing price at every 15 minute interval is captured. Similarly, in a daily chart, the daily closing price is recorded. Figures 8.1(a) and (b) show a market price signal simulated as a pure sine wave. The sine wave in Fig. 8.1(a) was sampled at eight points per cycle, yielding a sampled signal of circular frequency of $\pi/4$ radian (i.e., 45 degrees). If the horizontal axis is taken to be time in minutes, the figure can be considered as a 15-minute chart. Taking every other sample of Fig. 8.1(a) will yield Fig. 8.1(b), which shows a sine wave sampled at four points per cycle, yielding a sampled signal of circular frequency of $\pi/2$ radians (i.e., 90 degrees). Figure 8.1(b) can then be considered as a 30-minute chart. The procedure of taking every M^{th} sample point is called downsampling, which will be discussed in more detail in Appendix 6.

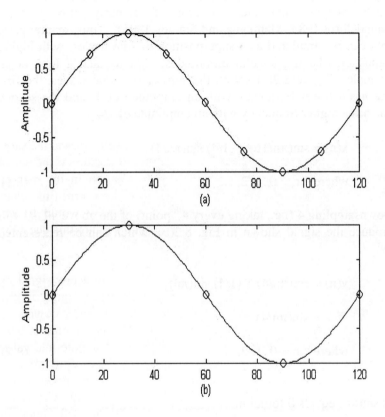

Fig. 8.1(a) A sine wave sampled at eight points per cycle; (b) taking every other sample of (a) yields a sine wave sampled at four points per cycle.

Market price data are seldom made up of a pure sine wave. They are usually composed of waves of different frequencies and magnitudes. In general, data of higher frequencies (i.e., smaller periods) have smaller amplitude than those of lower frequencies (i.e., larger periods). For example, the variation of daily closing price is much smaller than the variation of monthly closing price (Mandelbrot 1983, Mantegna and Stanley 1995). Thus, market price data can be simulated as a superposition of sine waves, with higher frequencies having smaller amplitudes. Let us take a look at an example. Figure 8.2(a) shows the sum of two sine waves, the first one has a lower frequency with an amplitude of 1, and the second one has a higher frequency with an amplitude of 1/4:

$$x(n) = \sin(\pi n/16) + (1/4)\sin(\pi n/4)$$

where $n = 0, 1, 2, \ldots$ (8.1)

Downsampling 4 (i.e., taking every 4th point) of the above signal will produce the signal shown in Fig. 8.2(b), which can be represented by:

$$v(n) = \sin(\pi n/4) + (1/4)\sin(\pi n)$$

$$= \sin(\pi n/4)$$

where $n = 0, 1, 2, \ldots$ (8.2)

as $\sin(\pi n)$ equals 0 for all n.

Thus, downsampling 4 as represented in Fig. 8.2(b) provides the perfect low pass filter, filtering off completely the signal of higher frequency. Furthermore, it does not alter the amplitude of the signal of the lower frequency, nor does it change its phase.

However, it should be noted that the filtered signal is affected by the initial point of downsampling. For example, if that

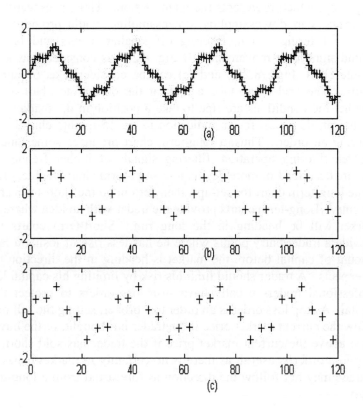

Fig. 8.2(a) Market data simulated as the sum of two sine waves; (b) Signal in (a) is downsampled by taking every 4th point; (c) Signal in (a) is downsampled by taking every 4th point, but the points are shifted by two positions as compared to (b).

point is shifted, as shown in Fig. 8.2(c), the filter will not be a perfect filter. Part of the signal of the higher frequency is not filtered off. But, in spite of that, we can still see mainly the wave of the lower frequency, which represents the major action. Thus, irrespective of where we start downsampling, downsampling would provide some kind of filtering action, filtering off smaller events and leaving behind significant movements. If Fig. 8.2(a) is considered as a 15-minute chart, Figs. 8.2(b) and (c) can be considered as 60-minute charts. The trader can take a look at the 60-minute chart to see whether the conditions are ripe to take a position in the market. He or she can then wait for an indication in the 15-minute chart before entering an order. Thus, a long-term chart produces some kind of lag-free filtering operation, filtering signals of higher frequencies that are described in more details in a short-term chart. Traders look at the long-term chart for set-ups, then zero in on the short-term chart for entry. Long-term charts provide the trader with an idea where the market will be heading in the long run. Short-term charts will provide a trader entry points where he has less risk of losing a large amount of capital before the market is heading in the direction that he expects. A trader should limit his risk by limiting his capital loss. Professional traders usually have stop loss orders to protect their capital. A stop loss order is an order to a broker, setting the sell price below the current market price if the trader has bought, or the buying price above the current market price if the trader has sold short. A stop loss order is useful, as there is no certainty in market behavior. A trade may not follow the direction as forecasted from a long-term chart.

8.1 Under-sampling

Before we apply an indicator on a sampled signal in a certain timeframe, we have to ensure that the signal is not under-sampled, i.e., there should be enough points to represent a cycle. In Chapter 4, we discussed the Nyquist Theorem, which states that in order to accurately reproduce a signal of a certain frequency, the signal has to be sampled at a rate greater than twice the frequency. That is, each cycle has to be sampled for more than two points, which is equivalent to saying that the sampling circular frequency has to be smaller than π radians. Figure 8.3(a) shows a sine wave with three cycles, sampled at four points per cycle, i.e., the sampled signal has a circular frequency of $\pi/2$ radians. If a trader decides then to sample every third point, as shown in Fig. 8.3(b) (e.g., convert a 10-minute chart to a 30-minute chart), one-and-a-half cycle is sampled for only two points. In other words, the sampling circular frequency will be $3\pi/2$ radians. According to the Nyquist Theorem, the signal cannot be represented accurately. The sampled signal can actually be misled to be believed that it is a signal of a lower frequency, which is shown in Fig. 8.3(c) as the sine wave with one cycle. As the cycle is sampled every quarter of a cycle, the misrepresented sampled signal has a circular frequency of $\pi/2$ radians. This is an example of aliasing, which results from sampling a signal less than twice per cycle (Proakis and Manolakis 1996). Aliasing introduces a signal that can be quite different from the original signal. If an indicator is applied to the sampled points, it will only lead to a misleading output response.

How can a trader recognize that the signal that he is analyzing is an aliased signal? First, in a certain time chart, he should identify a signal of his own interest. Then, he should compare that time chart with shorter-term time charts to see whether the signal maintains roughly the same shape in all time charts. In order to facilitate the comparison, computer trading programs should have an option to have different time frames lining up in a horizontal fashion, similar to the display in Fig. 8.3. This would allow the trader to quickly recognize whether a signal is under-sampled. If a signal in a certain time chart is under-sampled, then he should choose a shorter-term time chart where it is not. This would ensure that he is not analyzing an alias signal.

In order for a signal not to be under-sampled, all we need is two points per cycle. However, very often, we need more points than that to yield a good indicator response. As a general guideline, a cycle needs to have more than 4 points. An indicator response depends on how many points per cycle the signal is being sampled.

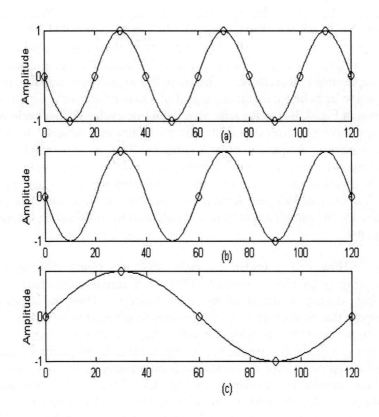

Fig. 8.3(a) A sine wave of three cycles sampled at four points per cycle; (b) taking every third sample of (a) yields a sine wave sampled at two points per one-and-a-half cycle; (c) the signal in (b) is under-sampled and would appear to look like a signal of a different frequency.

This is called its frequency characteristics. We will discuss this in the next section.

8.2 Frequency Characteristics of an Indicator

As discussed in Chapter 4, most indicators can be considered as filters in electrical engineering. The output response of a filter, which can be analyzed in terms of amplitude and phase, depends on the frequency of the signal. In trading, phase is more important than amplitude, as it represents the time lag of an indicator. In general, the lower the frequency (i.e., the more number of sampled points per cycle), the smaller the time lag, and the faster the indicator will respond. An example is shown in Figs. 6.7 and 6.8. In Fig. 6.7(a), the signal is sampled at 8 points per cycle, while in Fig. 6.8(a), the signal is sampled at 32 points per cycle. Thus, the signal in Fig. 6.8(a) has a lower frequency than the signal in Fig. 6.7(a). The cubic velocity indicator response of the signal shown in Fig. 6.8(b) has a slightly faster time response than that shown in Fig. 6.7(b). Similarly, but more obviously, the cubic accelerator indicator response of the signal shown in Fig. 6.8(c) has a much faster time response than that shown in Fig. 6.7(c). A much faster time response would mean that the trader could react faster to the behavior of the market. A signal with 32 points per cycle in a 15-minute time chart would become a signal with 8 points per cycle in a 60-minute time chart. The same indicator applying to the signals would yield a slightly faster response in the 15-minute time chart than that in the 60-minute time chart. The time response would vary from indicator to indicator. Frequency characteristics of some of the indicators are shown in Appendices 3 and 4.

Chapter 9

Wavelet Analysis

Wavelet analysis is a mathematical technique introduced in the nineteen eighties. Before then, signals are quite often analyzed by using Fourier Analysis. The Fourier Theorem states that every signal, no matter how complicated it may look, can be reproduced by adding a sufficient number of periodic curves called sine waves. Each sine wave has its own frequency and amplitude. In addition to how a signal can be synthesized, any arbitrary signal can also be analyzed. This is performed by using a certain filtering procedure to find out how much a particular sine wave contributes to a signal. The resulting list of sine waves is called the Fourier representation of a signal. Sine waves are periodic, and they go on and on forever. They are thus ideal for long, regular signals. However, sine waves do not cope well with signals of short duration. For a narrow spike, Fourier Analysis yields a very large number of sine waves of high frequencies, each of very long duration. When these sine waves are added together, they cancel each other out except at one point where they interfere constructively, creating the spike. Each sine wave component, taking individually, cannot pinpoint the timing of the spike.

This weakness of Fourier Analysis can be improved by using a procedure called windowed Fourier Analysis, where the signal is divided into a sequence of finite time slots called windows, and Fourier representation is found for each slot. However, as each window has a fixed, finite length, it is still not possible to locate a sharp spike very precisely. We would know which window the spike belongs to, but not exactly where it happens within the window.

Wavelet Analysis uses a flexible time window, and special mathematically designed waves called wavelets that can be stretched and translated in both frequency and time. The wavelets narrow while focusing on high frequency signals, and widen while searching for low frequency background. As a result, the frequency of the low frequency components are accurately defined at the expense of poor time localization. On the contrary, high frequency bands are precisely determined in time, but their frequencies are not well resolved (Lau and Weng 1995). This, however, is exactly what traders would like to see. They would like to know the long term trend from the low frequency background. At the same time, they would like to know the exact timing which can be extracted from high frequency signals when they would like to enter the market. As well, the wavelet approach is particularly appropriate in handling very irregular non-stationary data series. It deals well with signals of short duration, like bubbles and crashes.

In Chapter 5, we pointed out that trending indicators are actually low pass filters. They block out high frequency components of signals such as whipsaws but allow low frequency components of signals to go through. In other words, they smooth out the signals such that the traders would realize where the market is trending. In Chapter 6, we pointed out that oscillator indicators are high pass filters. They block out low frequency components such as trends and transmit high frequency components. They are used to find out the change of trend. Wavelets can be considered as band pass filters. They eliminate the very low frequencies and the very high frequencies and transmit the middle range frequencies. This is like keeping the middle layers of an onion. The middle layers can be further separated into different layers by adjusting the width of the wavelets. Unlike Fourier Analysis, which uses only sine waves as analyzing waves, wavelets come in different forms. Here, we will employ the sinc wavelet, which is one of the commonly used wavelets, to analyze market price data. The width of the wavelet is changed such that it can filter out different range of frequencies. Three ranges of frequencies will be chosen. We will call these filters as high, middle and low wavelet indicators.

9.1 High Wavelet Indicator

The high wavelet indicator is a band pass filter which will transmit high circular frequency of the range between $\pi/8$ and $\pi/4$ radian, which corresponds to periods of 16 bars and 8 bars respectively. Its coefficients are given by

$$h_{-3}(k) = \frac{1}{\pi k}\left(\sin\frac{\pi k}{4} - \sin\frac{\pi k}{8}\right) \qquad k = 0,1,2,3,... \qquad (9.1)$$

Its derivation is given in Appendix 7. The values of its coefficients are plotted in Fig. 9.1 and listed in Appendix 7. The number of coefficients are arbitrarily chosen to be 121 (i.e., k = 120). For k larger than 120, the coefficients are much smaller than those where k are less than 120, and therefore ignored. The subscript '-3' of h is a certain way to identify the wavelet indicator and will be explained in Appendix 7.

9.2 Middle Wavelet Indicator

The middle wavelet indicator is a band pass filter which will transmit middle circular frequency of the range between $\pi/16$ and $\pi/8$ radian, which corresponds to periods of 32 bars and 16 bars respectively. Its coefficients are given by

$$h_{-4}(k) = \frac{1}{\pi k}\left(\sin\frac{\pi k}{8} - \sin\frac{\pi k}{16}\right) \qquad k = 0,1,2,3,... \qquad (9.2)$$

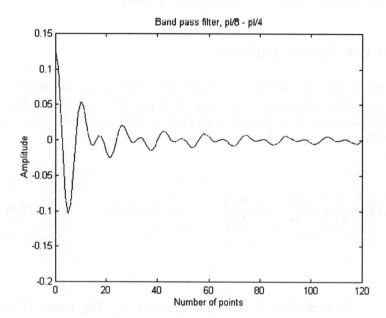

Fig. 9.1. Coefficients of the high wavelet indicator.

Its derivation is given in Appendix 7. The values of its coefficients are plotted in Fig. 9.2 and listed in Appendix 7. The number of coefficients are arbitrarily chosen to be 121 (i.e., k = 120). For k larger than 120, the coefficients are much smaller than those where k are less than 120, and therefore ignored.

9.3 Low Wavelet Indicator

The low wavelet indicator is a band pass filter which will transmit low circular frequency of the range between $\pi/32$ and $\pi/16$ radian, which corresponds to periods of 64 bars and 32 bars respectively. Its coefficients are given by

$$h_{-5}(k) = \frac{1}{\pi k}\left(\sin\frac{\pi k}{16} - \sin\frac{\pi k}{32}\right) \qquad k = 0,1,2,3,... \qquad (9.3)$$

Its derivation is given in Appendix 7. The values of its coefficients are plotted in Fig. 9.3 and listed in Appendix 7. The number of coefficients are arbitrarily chosen to be 201 (i.e. k = 200). For k larger than 200, the coefficients are much smaller than those where k are less than 200, and therefore ignored.

These wavelet indicators can be used to resolve market price data within one time frame into different frequency components. These can be compared to using trending indicators on various time frames (Note that trending indicators are low pass filters and always leave the low frequency background of the signal in the filtered signal). Thus, wavelet indicators offer traders the advantage of looking at market movements within one time frame but seeing the slow and fast activities simultaneously.

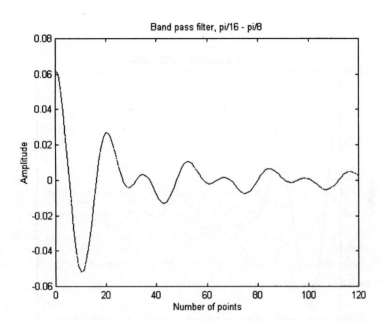

Fig. 9.2. Coefficients of the middle wavelet indicator.

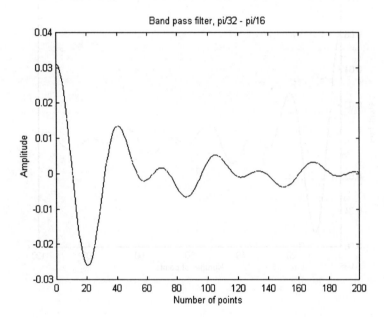

Fig. 9.3. Coefficients of the low wavelet indicator.

We will first take a look at how a high wavelet indicator can filter out the low frequency component of a signal, and how a cubic velocity indicator will act on the filtered signal as to indicate the peaks and valleys of the high frequency signal. Figure 9.4(a) shows a sine wave p1 of high frequency (circular frequency = $\pi/6$) and a sine wave p2 of low frequency (circular frequency = $\pi/16$) and their sum. The sum signal is then filtered by the high wavelet indicator (which will filter off the low frequency signal), and the filtered signal is then operated on by the cubic velocity indicator. The final result agrees reasonably well with the theoretical result shown in Fig. 9.4(b), where the derivative (or slope) of p1 is plotted. This shows that the high wavelet indicator can filter away the low frequency component of the signal quite well. The cubic velocity indicator can then help to identify the top and bottom of this high frequency component. However, it should be mentioned that the agreement depends on the frequency of the signal being analyzed, as wavelet indicators, just like any other indicators, can shift the filtered signal from the original signal in time or phase.

Figure 9.5 shows a 5-minute chart of an US 30 year Treasury Bond Future. The top plot displays market price as well as its smoothing by ama1 (thin line) and ama3 (thick line). These ama lines are plotted for references only. The middle plot shows the cubic velocity indicator applied to the market closing price data after they have been filtered by the high (thick line), middle (middle thick line), and low (thin line) wavelet indicators. The bottom plot shows the summation of the amplitudes of all these three lines. This bottom plot can be considered as filtering the data with a band pass filter between $\pi/32$ and $\pi/4$ and then applying a cubic velocity indicator on the filtered data.

At 9:50 a.m., the middle plot shows that all three lines are pointing up, providing a good entry point to go long in the market. At 12:50 p.m., the thin line is approximately zero and pointing down, implying that the long term trend is over. However, at that moment, the thick and middle thick line are positive and pointing up

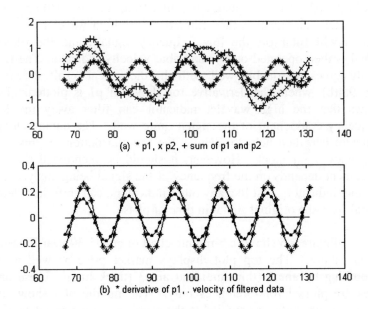

(a) * p1, x p2, + sum of p1 and p2

(b) * derivative of p1, . velocity of filtered data

Fig. 9.4(a) shows the sum (marked as +) of a high frequency sine wave p1 (marked as *) and a low frequency sine wave p2 (marked as x); (b) the sum signal is filtered by the high wavelet indicator and then operated on by the cubic velocity indicator. This signal (marked as .) is then compared to the derivative (or slope) of p1 (marked as *).

Fig. 9.5. A 5-minute chart of an US 30 year Treasury Bond Future. The middle plot shows the cubic velocity indictor applied to the market closing price data after they have been filtered by the high (thick line), middle (middle thick line), and low (thin line) wavelet indicators. The bottom plot shows the summation of the amplitudes of all these three lines. *Chart produced with Omega Research TradeStation2000i.*

at the same time, showing that the bulls are coming back to support the market. At 2:50 p.m., the three lines are either negative or approximately zero and pointing down, indicating a good point to exit the market.

In this wavelet analysis, the very high (higher than $\pi/4$ radians) and very low (lower than $\pi/32$ radians) frequencies have been eliminated. Wavelet indicators, can, however, be constructed to include some of the very high, or some of the very low frequencies, if needed. Thus, wavelet indicators would form an efficient way to monitor a market in one time frame by dividing the signal into different frequency components. Nevertheless, they do have certain disadvantages. A large number of coefficients are required to perform good filtering in order to transmit certain frequency bands. Since frequency in market price data changes quite fast, a large number of coefficients will contribute some inaccuracy in the filtering. In addition, except at certain frequencies where there are no phase lags, wavelet indicators do introduce a certain amount of phase lag. The phase lags would be described in more detail in Appendix 7.

Chapter 10

Other New Techniques

Two new ideas will be presented in this chapter to facilitate traders to make their decisions earlier so that they would have an advantage over other traders.

10.1 Skipped Convolution

Traders usually take specific market action from a chosen time frame and make certain judgement. For example, if a trader has a habit to trade in a 15-minute time frame, he will wait until the end of every 15 minutes (or near the end of every 15 minutes if his trading program can update the indicators every tick, a tick being the upward or downward price movement in a security's trades) before he makes a decision whether to enter a market. However, the market action can arrive 5 or 10 minutes earlier. It would, therefore, definitely be an advantage to recognize the action a few minutes earlier than other traders who are trading at the 15-minute time frame. What we can do is to use a 5-minute time frame, but analyze the signal in every 15-minute time interval. In that case, we would know the market action of the 15-minute time frame, but in every 5 minutes. We will introduce here a concept that will allow the trader to analyze the signal from a smaller time frame but using a larger time frame interval. The concept is called skipped convolution whose mathematical details will be described in Appendix 8.

For an indicator with coefficients $h(0)$, $h(1)$, $h(2)$ and $h(3)$, its output response after convoluting with the market data is given by

$$y(0) = h(0)x(0) + h(1)x(-1) + h(2)x(-2) + h(3)x(-3) \qquad (10.1)$$

where $x(0)$ is the closing price or the smoothed closing price of the current bar

$x(-1)$ is the closing price or the smoothed closing price of one bar ago

$x(-2)$ is the closing price or the smoothed closing price of two bars ago

$x(-3)$ is the closing price or the smoothed closing price of three bars ago

If this indicator is applied in the 5-minute chart, but we would like to see its output response as if it were in a 15 minute-chart, we can define the response in a skipped convolution with a skip 3:

$$y_3(0) = h(0)x(0) + h(1)x(-3) + h(2)x(-6) + h(3)x(-9) \qquad (10.2)$$

where　$x(-3)$ is the closing price or the smoothed closing price of three bars ago

$x(-6)$ is the closing price or the smoothed closing price of six bars ago

$x(-9)$ is the closing price or the smoothed closing price of nine bars ago

Equation (10.2) will give us the output response of the indicator as if it were in a 15-minute chart but at every 5-minute interval. This means that if a specific market action comes 5 minutes or 10 minutes after a 15-minute interval in a 15-minute chart, the trader using Eq (10.2) in a 5-minute chart will detect the action 5 minutes or 10 minutes earlier than the trader using the same indicator in a 15- minute chart.

If the indicator is applied in the 5-minute chart, but we would like to see its output response as if it were in a 60 minute chart, we can define the response in a skipped convolution with a skip 12:

$$y_{12}(0) = h(0)x(0) + h(1)x(-12) + h(2)x(-24) + h(3)x(-36) \qquad (10.3)$$

where $x(-12)$ is the closing price or the smoothed closing price of twelve bars ago

$x(-24)$ is the closing price or the smoothed closing price of twenty-four bars ago

$x(-36)$ is the closing price or the smoothed closing price of thirty-six bars ago

Equation (10.3) will give us the output response of the indicator as if it were in a 60-minute chart but at every 5-minute interval. This means that if a specific market action comes 5, 10, 15, ... 50, 55 minute after a 60-minute interval in a 60-minute chart, the trader using Eq (10.3) in a 5-minute chart will detect the action 5, 10, 15, ... 50, 55 minutes earlier than the trader using the same indicator in a 60-minute chart.

In the EasyLanguage code of Omega Research's TradeStation2000i, the program for calculating the skipped exponential moving average with a length of 3 can be written as a function as follows: -

```
Inputs: P(Numeric), D(Numeric);
emaL3D=
0.5*c[P+0]+0.25*c[P+D]+0.125*c[P+2*D]+0.0625*c[P+3*D]+0.03
```

12*c[P+4*D]+0.0156*c[P+5*D]+0.0078*c[P+6*D]+0.0039*c[P+7*
D]+0.0020*c[P+8*D]+0.0010*c[P+9*D]+0.0005*c[P+10*D]+0.000
2*c[P+11*D]+0.0001*c[P+12*D]+0.0001*c[P+13*D]

emaL3D is an exponential moving average function with length
equals to 3 and a skip parameter equals to D. When D = 1, it is the
same as an ordinary exponential moving average of length 3. The
input numeric parameter D allows the traders to skip analyzing price
data at a predetermined regular interval. P is another input numeric
parameter. It allows the trader to choose the bar P where he will start
smoothing the data. This last feature would be useful when an
indicator, e.g., cubic velocity indicator is applied to the smoothed
skipped data. The coefficients in the program is calculated from Eq
(A3.22) with M = 3 in Appendix 3.

For an exponential moving average of length equal to 6 and
a skip parameter equals to D, it can be written as a function in the
EasyLanguage code as follows:-

Inputs: P(Numeric), D(Numeric);
emaL6D=
0.2857*c[P+0]+0.2041*c[P+D]+0.1458*c[P+2*D]+0.1041*c[P+3*
D]+0.0744*c[P+4*D]+0.0531*c[P+5*D]+0.0379*c[P+6*D]+0.0271
*c[P+7*D]+0.0194*c[P+8*D]+0.0138*c[P+9*D]+0.0099*c[P+10*
D]+0.0071*c[P+11*D]+0.0050*c[P+12*D]+0.0036*c[P+13*D]+0.0
026*c[P+14*D]+0.0018*c[P+15*D]+0.0013*c[P+16*D]+0.0009*c[
P+17*D]+0.0007*c[P+18*D]+0.0005*c[P+19*D]+0.0003*c[P+20*
D]

The coefficients in the program is calculated from Eq (A3.22) with
M = 6 in Appendix 3.

After smoothing the data with an exponential moving
average in a skip fashion, we can apply an indicator to the smoothed
data if we choose. The indicator can be a skipped indicator. The
following program, written as an indicator in EasyLanguage code,
shows how to apply the skipped cubic velocity indicator on the
smoothed skipped data.

{Skipped cubic velocity indicator}
Inputs: D(Numeric);
Plot1(11*emaL3D(0,D)/6-3*emaL3D(D,D)+3*emaL3D(2*D,D)/2-
emaL3D(3*D,D)/3,"Plot1");
Plot2(11*emaL6D(0,D)/6-3*emaL6D(D,D)+3*emaL6D(2*D,D)/2-
emaL6D(3*D,D)/3,"Plot2");
Plot3(0,"Plot3");

In this program, D is an input parameter, which provides the skipping for the cubic velocity indicator. It should be noted that the skip parameter D of the skipped indicator has the same value as the skip parameter D of the exponential moving average functions. The first plot plots the response of the skipped cubic velocity indicator after the data has been skipped smoothed by an exponential moving average of length 3. The second plot plots the response of the skipped cubic velocity indicator after the data has been skipped smoothed by an exponential moving average of length 6. The third plot plots a horizontal straight line as a reference where the velocity is 0.

An example is given in Fig. 10.1, which shows a 5-minute chart of an US 30 year Treasury Bond Future. Exponential moving averages, ema3 and ema6 (see Chapter 5) with a skip 3 (D = 3 in emaL3D and emaL6D function programs) were first employed to smooth the market price. A cubic velocity indicator with a skip 3 convolution (D = 3 in the skipped cubic velocity indicator program) was employed to convolute with the smoothed skipped data. This is equivalent to getting a 15-minute chart response but in a 5-minute interval. The velocity responses (ema3, thin line; ema6, thick line) are shown in the middle plot. Exponential moving averages, ema3 and ema6, with a skip 12 ((D = 12 in emaL3D and emaL6D function programs), were also used to smooth the market price. A cubic velocity indicator with a skip 12 convolution (D = 12 in the skipped cubic velocity indicator program) was employed to convolute with the smoothed skipped data. This is equivalent to getting a 60-minute chart response but in a 5-minute interval. The velocity responses (ema3, thin line; ema6, thick line) are shown in the bottom plot.

Fig. 10.1. A 5-minute chart of an US 30 year Treasury Bond Future. The middle plot shows a skip 3 cubic velocity indictor applied to the market closing price data after they have been filtered by skip 3 exponential moving averages. The bottom plot shows a skip 12 cubic velocity indictor applied to the market closing price data after they have been filtered by skip 12 exponential moving averages. *Chart produced with Omega Research TradeStation2000i.*

At 11:10 a.m. (marked by an up arrow), the skip 3 velocities and the skip 12 velocities approached zero and pointed up. These implied that both the 15-minute traders and the 60-minute traders are bullish in the market. That signified a good buy entry point.

At 2:15 p.m. (marked by a down arrow), the skip 3 velocities and the skip 12 velocities approached zero and pointed down. These implied that both the 15-minute traders and the 60-minute traders are bearish on the market. That signified a good exit point. In both cases, we do not need to wait till the end of every 15 minutes or every 60 minutes to find out the indicator response in a 15-minute or 60-minute chart. We would know their response every 5 minutes, thus providing an advantage.

10.2 Forecasts

Traders would like to see forecasts of market values. You may run into a trading newsletter that claims that they can forecast what point the Dow Jones Industrial Average will be at a few years from now. However, market forecasting is a highly inaccurate exercise. It is even far less accurate than weather forecasting. The weather is a consequence of multiple forces in nature, which is complicated. The market is a consequence of thousands of human minds, which are even more complicated. In general, assuming if any event is forecastable at all, the farther the future is from the present moment, the larger the error would the forecast be. This is simply because events happening between the present and the forecasted future will affect the future being forecasted.

As the financial market has a highly unpredictable behavior, all traders can really hope for is that the actual market value lies within a certain % limit of the forecasted value ((Box, Jenkins and Reinsel 1994). We will suggest here a forecasting method that makes use of the cubic velocity indicator and the cubic acceleration indicator. Even though the method can be used to forecast market value a few bars ahead, it is expected that the error will be large.

Therefore, we will concentrate on forecasting market value only one bar ahead. This is called one-step-ahead forecast.

Using the cubic velocity indicator, the one-step-ahead forecast is given by

$$x(1) = \frac{17}{6}x(0) - 3x(-1) + \frac{3}{2}x(-2) + \frac{1}{3}x(-3) \qquad (10.4)$$

where   x(1) is the forecasted closing price one bar ahead

x(0) is the closing price or the smoothed closing price of the current bar

x(−1) is the closing price or the smoothed closing price one bar ago

x(−2) is the closing price or the smoothed closing price of two bars ago

x(−3) is the closing price or the smoothed closing price of three bars ago

The derivation of Eq (10.4) is given in Appendix 8.

Figure 10.2 shows a summation of two sine waves and the one-step-ahead forecast given by Eq (10.4). The forecasted values agree with the given values quite well.

A slightly modified forecasting method employs both the cubic velocity indicator and the cubic acceleration indicator. The one-step-ahead forecast is given by

$$x(1) = \frac{23}{6}x(0) - \frac{11}{2}x(-1) + \frac{7}{2}x(-2) - \frac{5}{6}x(-3) \qquad (10.5)$$

The derivation of Eq (10.5) is given in Appendix 8.

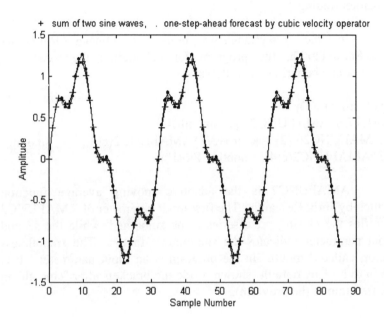

Fig. 10.2. A summation of sine waves (marked as +) of circular frequency of $\pi/16$ radian with amplitude 1.0 and $\pi/4$ radian with amplitude 0.25 . The one-step-ahead forecast (marked as .) using the cubic velocity indicator is also plotted.

Figure 10.3 shows a summation of two sine waves and the one-step-ahead forecast given by Eq (10.5). Again, the forecasting values agree with the given values quite well. While the agreements are better than those in Fig. 10.2 in some locations, the agreements are slightly worse than those in Fig. 10.2 in other locations. We therefore simply choose Eq (10.4) to be our one-step-ahead forecast in market trading.

In the EasyLanguage code of Omega Research's TradeStation2000i, the program for calculating the forecasting indicator can be written as follows: -

```
Input: smooth(1);
Plot1(17/6*AMAFUNC2(c[1],smooth)-
3*AMAFUNC2(c[2],smooth)+3/2*AMAFUNC2(c[3],          smooth)-
1/3*AMAFUNC2(c[4], smooth),"Plot1");
```

AMAFUNC2 is the adaptive moving average function written by Jurik Research. The first input parameter of AMAFUNC2 signifies the closing price series to be smoothed, while the second input parameter indicates the smoothness factor. The smoothness factor, called "smooth" in the program is an input parameter. It is taken to be 1 by default (shown inside the brackets after "smooth" in the first line of the program).

Figure 10.4 shows a 5-minute chart of the US 30 year Treasury Bond Future. An adaptive moving average with smoothness 1 (ama1) was used to average the closing price and is shown in a thin line. The one-step-ahead forecasted values are plotted in dashes and agreed reasonably with the closing prices they predicted.

The forecasting model described here is a simple model of what may happen. More sophisticated forecasting model, which analyses the frequency content of the data, has been described by Santana and Mendes (1992). Forecasting is performed using on-line adaptive filter predictors. However, market behavior can change drastically at a moment's notice. Any forecasting model should, at best, be looked upon as only some kind of guidance. Also, the forecasted value should include errors of estimation.

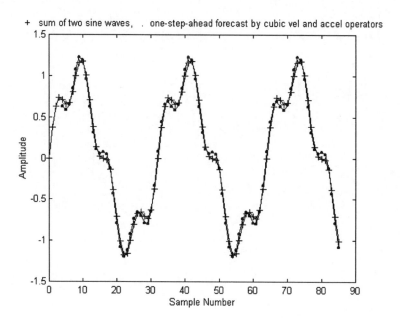

Fig. 10.3. A summation of sine waves (marked as +) of circular frequency of $\pi/16$ radian with amplitude 1.0 and $\pi/4$ radian with amplitude 0.25 . The one-step-ahead forecast (marked as .) using the cubic velocity and acceleration indicators is also plotted.

Fig. 10.4. A 5-minute chart of an US 30 year Treasury Bond Future. The one-step-ahead forecast using the cubic velocity indicator are plotted in dashes. *Chart produced with Omega Research TradeStation2000i.*

Chapter 11

Trading Systems

Among traders, there are many who are system traders. A system trader follows a set of rules which make up the system. He is consistent and does not deviate from the system's rules at any time. The rules will dictate when he will enter and when he will exit the market. (The meaning of systems here is different from that of systems in digital signal processing as described in Appendix 2.)

There are quite a number of commercial trading systems guaranteed to make profits. They come in manuals or CD-ROM, and some cost more than a few thousand dollars each. Quite often, it is not clear why the system sellers arrive at their rules and what justifications do they have, if any. Many system buyers got burned. A trader can develop his own system. But he should attempt to understand the basic assumptions and hypotheses behind each system and try to find out what restrictions it has.

Indicators provide the tools for building a system. As in cooking, we need tools to do the work. However, we still need a good recipe to make a good dish. A good trading system is a good recipe. Without it, no money can be made.

A trading system should be first tested on theoretical data and then on the real data. How should we make up the theoretical data as to simulate the market price data? As the market is changing all the time, we can only expect to model the market piecemeal. Traders quite often describe the market to be in cycle mode or trending mode. A cycle mode is when the price moves up and down.

A trending mode is when the price has a sustained large increase or decrease. The classification into these two modes is, of course, an approximation. But, then again, all models are. We will look for theoretical data to represent those modes. In Chapter 4, we mentioned that any practical signal could be expressed as a Fourier series, which is a sum of a number of sine waves. Thus, the simplest appropriate theoretical data would be a single sine wave, which simulate the market in a cycle mode. A slightly more complicated theoretical data would be the sum of two sine waves, with smaller waves superimposed on a larger wave. From the perspective of the smaller waves, the large wave is trending up and down. Thus, it can be said that part of the data is in trending mode. Modeling the market with more than two sine waves is, of course, possible. However, as described in Chapter 8, down-sampling can filter off some higher frequencies. So, to keep things simple, within a certain timeframe, we can take theoretical data to be at most two sine waves.

After testing the system on theoretical data and make sure that it is profitable, the trader should test the system on some past financial data and ensure that it is also profitable. In spite of that, there is no guarantee that the system will be profitable for future financial data. This is simply because real financial data is difficult to model and forecast. All a trader can hope for is to work out a system that will give him a better edge of winning.

Some traders attempt to create different trading systems to trade on the cycle and trending modes. This, of course, would mean that the trader would have to know a priori which mode the market will be in. This can be difficult. However, as described in Chapter 6, the cubic velocity and the cubic acceleration indicators have the potential to differentiate which mode the market is in. Other methods of indications have also been suggested by Ehlers (1992).

When the market is in a cycle mode within a certain timeframe, the strategy would be simple. All a trader needs to do is to identify the market tops and bottoms. This can be done using the cubic velocity indicator as described in Chapter 6. A trading system can be built around this indicator.

When the market is in a trending mode, probably two timeframes should be used. The long term timeframe is employed to ensure that the market is trending. The short term timeframe is used to look for entry points when the market retraces. Thus, during uptrends in the long term charts, the trader can look for declines in the short term charts to find buying opportunities. During downtrends in the long term charts, the trader can look for rallies in the short term charts to find shorting opportunities. This can be done by using both the cubic velocity and cubic acceleration indicators described in Chapter 6. What factor should be used to link the long term and short term timeframes? A factor of five is most common. Traders use, for example, daily and weekly charts as there are five trading days in a week (Elder 1993). However, this all depends on what are the periods of the smaller wave and the larger wave. A factor of four may provide better details.

Trading systems can be designed to use multiple timeframes. The Triple Screen trading system proposed by Elder (1993) uses three. The first screen identifies the market tide. The second screen identifies a wave that goes against the tide, and the third screen identifies the ripples in the direction of the tide. For example, the first screen can be a weekly chart, the second screen would be a daily chart and the third screen a 60-minute chart. In the first screen, the weekly trend would be identified using a trending indicator, and the trader would only trade in this direction. In the second screen, an oscillator indicator would be applied to a daily chart. The trader would use daily declines during weekly uptrends to look for buying opportunities, and daily rallies during weekly downtrends to look for shorting possibilities. In the third screen, a trailing buy-stop would be applied in the uptrends and a trailing sell-stop would be applied in downtrends. Trailing buy-stop would catch upside breakouts, and trailing sell-stop would catch downside breakouts. This system works best when small waves are superimposed on a large wave.

Just as no scientific model can always accurately forecast a physical phenomenon, no system can precisely predict which direction the market is heading. While most models describing the behaviors of physical phenomena are deterministic models, models explaining market movements are probabilistic or stochastic models. As there are so many unknown factors involved, it is impossible to forecast the future value of any market price with a predetermined accuracy. A news item can completely throw the market off any course of expectation. Thus, all a trader can hope for is to design a system to give him or her better odds of winning. He or she may find certain indicators that will tell ahead of time what most other people will be doing. Indicators are mathematical constructs and have limitations. As such, it is very important that traders should include money management with their systems. Traders should put stop loss orders together with their buy or sell orders, in case the market is heading in a direction that they do not expect. The stop loss would protect their capital. Professional traders usually limit their loss to two percent of their equity in a single trade. If the market is heading in their favor, trailing stop loss orders should be put to protect any profit.

A good trading system, together with money management, can increase the probability of a trader's profitability.

Chapter 12

Financial Markets are Complex

After describing the market and indicators in all these pages, we are left with the impressions that financial market problems are not easy to solve. Why is it so, and what exactly is the market?

The financial market is a complex adaptive system, which is studied under the discipline of complexity theory. Concentrated effort in research in complexity theory started in the mid-1980s (Waldrop 1992). The theory has been employed to model and forecast the traffic density of various freeways at rush-hour traffic (Casti, 1996), how many people will be going to a certain bar next week (Casti 1996), and who is going to win the Super Bowl (Casti 1997b). Some believe that the theory is the science for the twenty-first century. The financial market is a typical example of a complex system. There, a number of traders and investors act independently in deciding whether to trade or stay away. These people are intelligent and adaptive. They make decisions and take actions on the basis of certain rules and systems. Furthermore, they are ready to modify their rules and systems on the basis of new knowledge. Market price moves in response to the decision making of all these traders.

As the crowd's decision making is the reason behind market movement, we can claim that we understand the market better than the appearance of sunspots in the sun. The formation of sunspots is still not very clear. If only we can monitor the brain waves of all traders, the market will be deterministic, at least for the next instant. However, as we cannot tap into the brains of the traders, the market has an unpredictable element. We can, however, hope that we can

134

average out the majority of the trader's thinking and do some forecasting, knowing that the forecast would contain certain errors.

Traders can be classified in general as fundamentalists and technical analysts. Fundamentalists rely on variables like company earnings, assets, new products, etc., to make their decision. This approach is more suitable for people trading stocks. Technical analysts rely on analyzing past price movements to decide whether to buy or sell or to stay out. This approach appeals to traders who trade commodities and index futures. As the only variable in this case is the past price, it would imply that future price depends only on past price, rendering the price series not so random. On the other hand if most traders trading a certain market are fundamentalists, future price movements would not depend on past price and the price series should be random. This, of course, should be the case, as non-randomness, mathematically speaking, relates to the correlation among prices.

Assuming most traders trading a certain market are technical analysts and employ price data only, the problem of forecasting the market would be much simplified, as the only input to the problem situation would be past prices.

Many indicators, which employ prices, have been developed to indicate which direction the market is heading. Not all indicators are relevant. The trader should test them on theoretical waveforms to see whether they do describe market actions. Using indicators, a trader can design his own set of rules for forecasting purposes. The rules would form his trading system, which should be of the nature of kinematics as it attempts to portray how the market moves. He will try to satisfy his material needs by organizing himself through individual acts of buying and selling. No one is in charge or consciously planning the market movements. This is an example of a complex system undergoing spontaneous self-organization.

In a complex system, every person would have his own rules. As a matter of fact, if every person uses the same rule, the rule will not work. A simple example will be given. Drivers on highways form a complex system. They know the rule that the leftmost lane is the fast lane. However, if every driver moves to the fast lane, the fast lane would not be the fast lane any more. Thus, the rule will be self-defeating. In the financial market, if all traders use the same set of rules, and since there must be a time lag among traders entering the market, the first of the traders would find the rules self-fulfilling, and the last of the traders would find the rules self-defeating.

The market, being complex, is also adaptive. Each trader will actively modify his rules to his advantage. He will also drop some of the rules and add new ones as the market changes in speed and in style. Furthermore, he can create new rules that have never before been used. Thus, a trader who uses the same set of rules year after year would eventually find them unprofitable. Trading, just like any business, needs to be updated as circumstance changes. We do not expect a business strategy to work forever, so why would we expect a trading system to work for eternity?

It should also be noted that no rules or indicators are perfect. Rules and indicators can only increase one's odd of winning. There is always certain intrinsic randomness in people's decision making and therefore market behavior. Crowd behavior, because of its adaptive and time-dependent nature, cannot be 100% predictable. In this sense, the financial market is, forever, a complex problem.

Time Series Analysis

Time series analysis concerns with the building of stochastic (statistical) models for time series and their applications. This includes model estimation and forecasting.

Many empirical time series (e.g. stock prices) do not look as if they have fixed average (or mean). However, they exhibit homogeneity in the sense that one part of the series looks much like any other part. This homogeneous non-stationary behavior can be reduced to a stationary model by taking suitable difference of the series. The general model is called an autoregressive integrated moving average (ARIMA) process. But first, we will describe the autoregressive moving average model.

A1.1 Autoregressive Moving Average Model

The equation of the model for the autoregressive moving average (ARMA) process is (Box, Jenkins and Reinsel 1994, p92)

$$\varphi(B)z_{to} = \theta(B)a_t \qquad\qquad (A1.1)$$

where

$$z_{to} = z_t - \mu \qquad\qquad (A1.2)$$

z_t are observations made at equidistant time intervals

μ is the mean of the stochastic process and can be estimated by the sample mean of N data points

$$\bar{z} = \frac{1}{N} \sum_{t=1}^{N} z_t \qquad\qquad (A1.3)$$

B is a (backward) shift operator defined by

$$Bz_t = z_{t-1} \qquad\qquad (A1.4)$$

$\varphi(B)$ is an autoregressive operator

a_t is a series of independent "shocks" that are random drawings from a fixed probability distribution, usually Normal and has mean zero and variance σ^2

$\theta(B)$ is a moving average operator and can be written as an operator of order q

$$\theta(B) = 1 - \theta_1 B - \theta_2 B^2 - \dots - \theta_q B^q \qquad\qquad (A1.5)$$

θ_i is a weight parameter of the moving average operator.

   If the roots of $\varphi(B) = 0$ lie outside the unit circle, the ARMA process is stationary. If the roots of $\varphi(B) = 0$ lie inside or on the unit circle, the process is non-stationary. If some of the roots lie on the unit circle, the process represents a homogeneous non-stationary time series.

A1.2 Autoregressive Integrated Moving Average Model

When d of the roots of $\varphi(B) = 0$ are unity and the rest of the roots lie outside the unit circle, Eq (A1.1) can be expressed as

$$\varphi(B)z_{to} = \phi(B)(1-B)^d z_{to} = \phi(B)\nabla^d z_{to} = \theta(B)a_t \tag{A1.6}$$

Here $\varphi(B)$ is a non-stationary autoregressive operator while $\phi(B)$ is a stationary autoregressive operator and can be written as an operator of order p

$$\phi(B) = 1 - \phi_1 B - \phi_2 B^2 \text{—} - \phi_p B^p \tag{A1.7}$$

where ϕ_i is the weight parameter of the autoregressive operator

∇ is the background difference operator and can be written in terms of B, since

$$\nabla z_t = z_t - z_{t-1} = (1-B)z_t \tag{A1.8}$$

As $\nabla^d z_{to} = \nabla^d z_t$ for $d \geq 1$, the model can be written as

$$\phi(B)\nabla^d z_t = \theta(B)a_t \tag{A1.9}$$

This process is called an autoregressive integrated moving average (ARIMA) process, or ARIMA (p d q) when the orders of each operator need to be specified.

A1.2.1 *IBM Stock Price*

One hundred successive observations of the daily IBM stock prices for a period beginning in May 1961 was fitted to the ARIMA model, resulting in a model of order (0 1 1). The model is written as (Box, Jenkin and Reinsel 1994, p98)

$$\nabla z_t = (1+0.1B)a_t \tag{A1.10}$$

which can be approximated as (Box, Jenkin and Reinsel p157, 328)

$$\nabla z_t = a_t \tag{A1.11}$$

which is an example of the random walk model given by

$$z_t = z_{t-1} + \sum_{j=0}^{t-1} a_{t-j} \tag{A1.12}$$

Thus the best forecast of future values of the stock is very nearly today's price.

A1.2.2 *Dow-Jones Utilities Index*, Aug 28 – Dec 18, 1972

The fitted model for the Dow-Jones Utilities Index (Brockwell and Davis 1996, p141) is written as

$$(1 - 0.4219B)(\nabla z_t - 0.1336) = a_t \tag{A1.13}$$

Taking the altered time series to be (∇z_t - 0.1336) where 0.1336 is the mean of the slope ∇z_t, this model is an ARIMA (1 0 0) process.

The data can also be fitted to an ARIMA (1 1 0) process (Brockwell and Davis 1996, p161)

$$(1-0.4471B)\nabla z_t = a_t \tag{A1.14}$$

All these models imply that the Dow-Jones utilities Index is not random.

A1.3   Model in Terms of Previous Data

The ARIMA model, Eq (A1.9), can be re-written as a model using previous z's and the current shock a_t (Box, Jenkins and Reinsel 1994, p108)

$$z_t = \sum_{j=1}^{\infty} \pi_j z_{t-j} + a_t \tag{A1.15}$$

where the first term on the right hand side of the equation is a weighted average of previous values (π_j is the weight parameter). Even though theoretically, z_t depends on the remote past; in practice, it is dependent only to a few recent past values z_{t-j} of the time series. If n values are used, the model will be an ARIMA (n 0 0) process. The daily closing price of the S & P index over the course of the year 1992 has been modeled with an ARIMA (8 0 0) process (Hatamian 1995). This example has been described in more detail in Chapter 3.

Appendix 2

Signals and Systems

Digital signal processing is the study of the representation of signals in digital form, and of the processing of these signals. We will describe the concepts of a discrete-time signal and a discrete-time system.

A2.1 Discrete-time Signals

A discrete-time signal is an indexed sequence of numbers. Thus, a discrete-time signal, $x(n)$ is a function of an integer-valued variable, n. In this book, the independent variable, n, represents time and $x(n)$ is a function of time. The sequence could be finite or infinite. It can also be doubly infinite, i. e., the index n goes from $-\infty$ to $+\infty$. The sequence values $x(n)$ can be considered as the elements of a vector.

$$\mathbf{x} = (- x(N\text{-}1), x(N), x(N+1), - x(\text{-}1), x(0), x(1), x(2), -) \quad (A2.1)$$

Stock market prices is an example of a discrete-time signal. For real time applications, where future data is not available, the vector can be written as

$$\mathbf{x} = (- x(N\text{-}1), x(N), x(N+1), - x(\text{-}1), x(0)) \quad\quad (A2.2)$$

A2.2 Discrete-time Systems

A discrete-time system, T, is an operator or a mapping that transforms the input signal, $x(n)$, into the output signal, $y(n)$, by means of a fixed set of operations

$$y(n) = T[x(n)] \tag{A2.3}$$

A system is linear if

$$T[a_1x_1(n)+a_2x_2(n)] = a_1T[x_1(n)]+a_2T[x_2(n)] \tag{A2.4}$$

for any two inputs $x_1(n)$ and $x_2(n)$ and for any constants a_1 and a_2 (Hayes 1999).

A system is shift-invariant if, for any delay n_0,

$$y(n-n_0) = T[x(n-n_0)] \tag{A2.5}$$

A system that is both linear and shift-invariant is described as a linear shift–invariant (LSI) system.

The output, $y(n)$, is related to the input, $x(n)$, of a linear shift-invariant system by the convolution sum (Hayes 1999, Strang and Nguyen 1997).

$$
\begin{aligned}
y(n) \\
&= h(n) * x(n) \\
&= - h(-1)x(n+1) + h(0)x(n) + h(1)x(n-1) + - \\
&= \sum_{k=-\infty}^{\infty} h(k)x(n-k)
\end{aligned} \tag{A2.6}
$$

which provides a complete characterization of an LSI system where $h(k)$ is the unit sample (or impulse) response (Hayes 1999).

The convolution operator satisfies the associative property, which is

$$[h_2(n)*h_1(n)]*x(n) = h_2(n)*[h_1(n)*x(n)] \qquad (A2.7)$$

This property is useful when a second indicator is applied on the data which has been operated on by an indicator.

For real-time applications, causality is an important system property. A system is described as causal if the response of the system at time n_0 depends only on the input up to the time $n = n_0$. An LSI system is causal if $h(n)$ is equal to zero for $n < 0$. For a causal system, the convolution sum can be written as

$$
\begin{aligned}
y(n) &= h(n)*x(n) \\
&= h(0)x(n) + h(1)x(n-1) + h(2)x(n-2) + - \\
&= \sum_{k=0}^{\infty} h(k)x(n-k)
\end{aligned}
\qquad (A2.8)
$$

Most trading indicators are causal systems. Every causal linear operator acting on the signal vector $\mathbf{x}$ can be represented by a matrix $\mathbf{H}$ (Strang and Nguyen 1997).

$$\mathbf{y} = \mathbf{Hx} \qquad (A2.9)$$

or

$$
\begin{bmatrix} \cdot \\ y(-1) \\ y(0) \\ y(1) \\ \cdot \end{bmatrix} = \begin{bmatrix} \cdot & \cdot & & \cdot & \cdot \\ \cdot & h(0) & & \cdot & \cdot \\ \cdot & h(1) & h(0) & & \cdot \\ \cdot & h(2) & h(1) & h(0) & \cdot \\ \cdot & \cdot & \cdot & \cdot & \cdot \end{bmatrix} \begin{bmatrix} \cdot \\ x(-1) \\ x(0) \\ x(1) \\ \cdot \end{bmatrix}
\qquad (A2.10)
$$

A2.3   Frequency Response of Linear Shift-invariant Systems

Eigenfunction of a system, T, is a mathematical function, or sequence which, when inputed to the system, outputs with only a change in complex amplitude. If the input is $x(n)$, the output $y(n)$ is written as

$$
y(n) = T[x(n)] = \lambda x(n) \qquad (A2.11)
$$

where λ is the eigenvalue and $x(n)$ is the eigenfunction. Signals of the form $x(n) = \exp(in\omega)$ are eigenfunctions of LSI systems. (ω is the circular frequency and is equal to 2π times frequency. It has a unit of radians. i is equal to $\sqrt{-1}$.) This can be shown from the convolution sum in Eq (A2.6) :

$$
\begin{aligned}
y(n) &\\
&= \sum_{k=-\infty}^{\infty} h(k)x(n-k) \\
&= \sum_{k=-\infty}^{\infty} h(k)\exp[i\omega(n-k)] \\
&= H[\exp(i\omega)]\exp(in\omega)
\end{aligned}
\qquad (A2.12)
$$

Thus, an LSI system has a pure frequency response to a pure frequency input (Strang and Nguyen 1997, Hayes 1999).

H[exp(iω)], which can be written as H(ω), is the eigenvalue and is given by

$$H(\omega) = \sum_{k=-\infty}^{k=\infty} h(k) \exp(-ik\omega) \qquad (A2.13)$$

H(ω) is the frequency response of an LSI system. It can also be considered as the Discrete Time Fourier Transform (DTFT) of the unit sample response h(k) (Haynes 1999, Oppenheim *et al* 1999). H(ω) is always periodic (Strang and Nguyen 1997).

$$H(\omega+2\pi) = H(\omega) \qquad (A2.14)$$

as exp(-ik2π) = 1.

The sequence h(k) can be represented by a Fourier integral called the Inverse Discrete Time Fourier Transform (Oppenheim *et al* 1999).

$$h(k) = \frac{1}{2\pi} \int_{-\pi}^{\pi} H(\omega) \exp(i\omega k) \, d\omega \qquad (A2.15)$$

H(ω) is usually complex and has a real and imaginary part:

$$H(\omega) = H_R(\omega) + iH_I(\omega) \qquad (A2.16)$$

Writing it in terms of its magnitude and phase

$$H(\omega) = |H(\omega)|\exp[i\phi(\omega)] \qquad (A2.17)$$

where

$$|H(\omega)| = \sqrt{[H_R^2(\omega) + H_I^2(\omega)]} \qquad (A2.18)$$

and

$$\phi(\omega) = \tan^{-1}\frac{H_I(\omega)}{H_R(\omega)} \qquad (A2.19)$$

Plots of magnitude and phase of $H(\omega)$ will be presented later. If $H(\omega)$ is real, $\phi(\omega) = 0$, and there is no phase shift. An example of real $H(\omega)$ is when the unit sample response is symmetric, i.e., $h(-k) = h(k)$. $H(\omega)$ will then be given by

$$H(\omega) = h(0) + 2\sum_{k=1}^{\infty} h(k)\cos(k\omega) \qquad (A2.20)$$

The frequency response of a causal LSI system is given by

$$H(\omega) = \sum_{k=0}^{\infty} h(k)\exp(-ik\omega) \qquad (A2.21)$$

which is usually complex.. An example of a complex $H(\omega)$, the frequency response of the sinc wavelet filter for a causal system, will be described in Appendix 7.

The frequency response $H(\omega)$ can show how a complex exponential is transformed when it is filtered by the system. It is especially useful if an input signal, $x(n)$, can be decomposed into a sum of complex exponentials,

$$x(n) = \sum_{k=1}^{N} a_k \exp(in\omega_k) \qquad\qquad (A2.22)$$

which is also known as a discrete time Fourier series expressed in exponential form (Brigham 1974). The response of an LSI system to this input will be given by

$$y(n) = \sum_{k=1}^{N} a_k \, H[\exp(i\omega_k)]\exp(in\omega_k) \qquad\qquad (A2.23)$$

As we will be dealing with sine waves as input in our financial model, we will take a look and see what is the response to this input will be. Let $x_0(n) = \sin(n\omega)$ be the input to an LSI system with a real-valued unit sample response $h(n)$. $x_0(n)$ can be written as

$$x_0(n) = \frac{1}{2i}\exp(in\omega) - \frac{1}{2i}\exp(-in\omega) \qquad\qquad (A2.24)$$

The response of the system can be written as

$$y_0(n) = \frac{1}{2i} H[\exp(i\omega)]\exp(in\omega) - \frac{1}{2i} H[\exp(-i\omega)]\exp(-in\omega) \quad \text{(A2.25)}$$

As h(n) is real-valued, $H[\exp(i\omega)]$ is conjugate symmetric:

$$H[\exp(-i\omega)] = H^*[\exp(i\omega)] \quad \text{(A2.26)}$$

Therefore,

$$
\begin{aligned}
y_0(n) \\
&= \frac{1}{2i} H[\exp(i\omega)]\exp(in\omega) - \frac{1}{2i} H^*[\exp(i\omega)]\exp(-in\omega) \\
&= \text{Im}\{H[\exp(i\omega)]\exp(in\omega)\} \\
&= |H[\exp(i\omega)]| \sin[n\omega + \phi(\omega)] \quad \text{(A2.27)}
\end{aligned}
$$

Thus a sine wave of frequency ω and of unit amplitude is transformed after filtering into a sine wave with the same frequency but with a phase shift and of amplitude equal to $|H[\exp(i\omega)]|$.

Technical analysts employ indicators to monitor the market. Indicators can provide insight into the balance of power between buying and selling. Traders should know what they measure and how they work. The amplitudes and phases of these indicators need to be understood.

Appendix 3

Low Pass Filters

A filter can be considered as a function of frequency. Signals of certain frequencies are allowed to pass through while others are blocked off. The output from a filter can be generated by convolving the input signal x(n) with a filter function or unit sample response h(k). The filter function is thus a linear shift-invariant (LSI) system, which is characterized by h(k). It can be divided into two types, those that have a finite-duration impulse response (FIR) and those that have an infinite-duration impulse response (IIR). An FIR system has an impulse response that is zero outside a certain finite time interval.

The convolution formula for a causal FIR system can be written as

$$y(n) = \sum_{k=0}^{N-1} h(k) x(n-k) \qquad\qquad (A3.1)$$

while the formula for a causal IIR system can be written as

$$y(n) = \sum_{k=0}^{\infty} h(k) x(n-k) \qquad\qquad (A3.2)$$

The most common types of filters are low-pass filters and high-pass filters. We will discuss low-pass filters in this Appendix and high-pass filters in the next.

Low-pass filters eliminate high frequency signals or noise. An example is the Simple Moving Average (SMA), which is quite often used by traders (Elders 1993).

A3.1 Simple Moving Average (SMA)

A simple N-day average is created by adding the prices over N days and dividing by N. It becomes a simple moving average when the next day's weighted price is added to the sum and the weighted first day's price is dropped off. It is thus given by Eq (A3.1) with

$$h(k) = 1/N \tag{A3.3}$$

Day, of course, can be replaced by any time unit. For example, a time unit can be a 15-minute time interval.

A3.1.1 *Two point Moving Average*

For a two point moving average, N = 2. From Eq (A3.1) and (A3.3) (Strang and Nguyen 1997, Hamming 1989)

$$y(n) = (1/2)x(n) + (1/2)x(n-1) \tag{A3.4}$$

The frequency response function $H(\omega)$ is, in the general case of N points, given by

(see Eq (A2.13))

$$H(\omega) = \sum_{k=0}^{N-1} h(k) \exp(-ik\omega) \tag{A3.5}$$

For the two point moving average,

$$H(\omega)=\frac{1}{2}+\frac{1}{2}\exp(-i\omega)=(\cos\frac{\omega}{2})\exp(-i\omega/2) \qquad \text{(A3.6)}$$

The magnitude and phase of $H(\omega)$ are

$$|H(\omega)|=\cos(\omega/2) \qquad \text{(A3.7)}$$

$$\phi(\omega)=-\omega/2 \qquad \text{(A3.8)}$$

The two point moving average has a phase delay which is linear with respect to ω. Graphs of amplitude and phase of the two point moving average are plotted in Fig. A3.1(a) and Fig. A3.1(b). A sine wave with $\pi/4$ radians/sample as well as its two point moving average are plotted in Fig. A3.2. The reduced amplitude and phase lag of the moving average are obvious. It should be noted that in trading, the phase of a filter (or indicator) is more important than its amplitude. A phase delay implies a time delay. A delay in time of executing an order can be costly.

A3.1.2 *N point Moving Average*

The output response of an N point moving average is given by

$$y(n)=\frac{1}{N}\sum_{k=0}^{N-1}x(n-k) \qquad \text{(A3.9)}$$

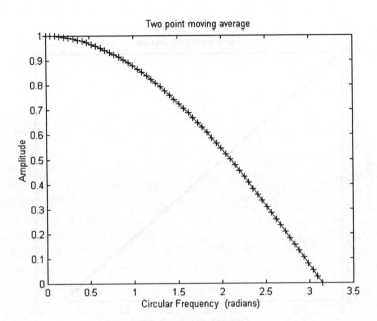

Fig. A3.1(a). Amplitude response of a two point moving average.

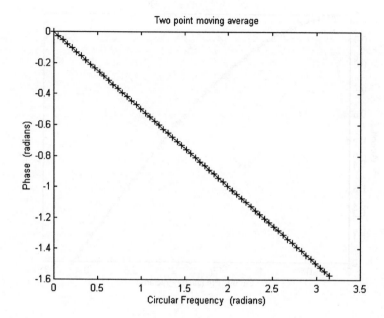

Fig. A3.1(b). Phase response of a two point moving average.

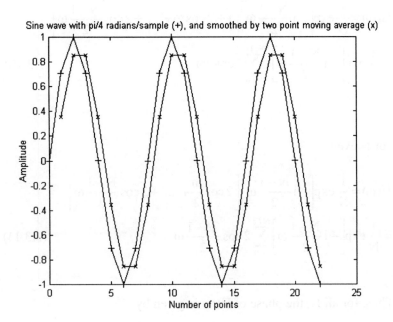

Fig. A3.2. A sine wave of circular frequency of $\pi/4$ radian (marked as +), and its output response after smoothed by a two point moving average (marked as x).

Using Eq (A3.5), the frequency response function $H(\omega)$ is given by

For N odd,

$$H(\omega) = \frac{1}{N}\exp\left[-i\frac{N-1}{2}\omega\right]\left[1 + 2\cos\omega + \ldots + 2\cos\frac{N-1}{2}\omega\right]$$

$$= \frac{1}{N}\exp\left[-i\frac{N-1}{2}\omega\right]\sum_{\ell=0}^{(N-1)/2} 2\cos\ell\omega \qquad (A3.10)$$

For N even

$$H(\omega) = \frac{1}{N}\exp\left[-i\frac{N-1}{2}\omega\right]\left[2\cos\frac{\omega}{2} + \ldots + 2\cos\frac{N-1}{2}\omega\right]$$

$$= \frac{1}{N}\exp\left[-i\frac{N-1}{2}\omega\right]\sum_{\ell=0}^{N/2} 2\cos\frac{2\ell-1}{2}\omega \qquad (A3.11)$$

Thus, for all N, the phase of $H(\omega)$ is given by

$$\phi(\omega) = -\frac{N-1}{2}\omega \qquad (A3.12)$$

which is linear with respect to ω.

The larger the number of points, N, the smoother the output response is. However, it will also yield a larger phase lag, according to Eq (A3.12). The amplitude and phase of the six point moving average filter are plotted in Figs. A3.3(a) and (b). In Fig. A3.3(b), the phase should have been linear. The jump in phase is caused by the build-in function arctan used to calculated $\phi(\omega)$ being defined only from $-\pi$ to π in the computer program.

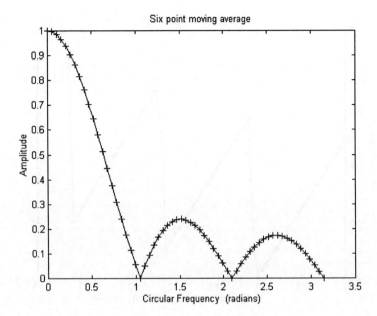

Fig. A3.3(a). Amplitude response of a six point moving average.

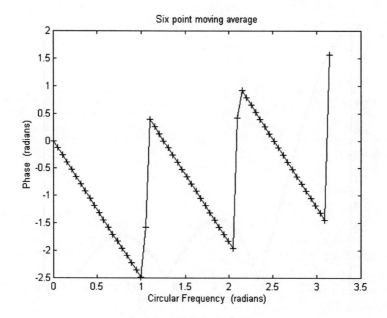

Fig. A3.3(b). Phase response of a six point moving average.

A3.2 Exponential Moving Average (EMA)

An exponential moving average(EMA) is a better tool than a simple moving average. It gives greater weight to the latest data and thus responds to changes faster. It does not drop old data suddenly the way an SMA does. Old data fades away.

The equation for the output response of an EMA is given by

$$y(n) = \alpha x(n) + (1-\alpha)y(n-1) \qquad (A3.13)$$

where $\alpha = 2/(M+1)$ $\qquad\qquad$ (A3.14)

M is a positive integer chosen by the trader and is often called the length of the EMA.

Equation (A3.13) makes use of an output response that has already been processed. Filters that employ previously processed values are sometimes called recursive filter. To calculate the frequency response of EMA, the z-transform of Eq (A3.13) is taken (Broesch 1997, Proakis and Manolakis 1996).

$$Y(z) = \alpha X(z) + (1-\alpha)z^{-1}Y(z) \qquad (A3.15)$$

where $z = r \exp(i\omega)$ is a complex number in the complex plane, r being the magnitude of z. $Y(z)$ is the transform of the output and $X(z)$ is the transform of the input.

Defining the transfer function as the output of the filter over the input of the filter

$$H(z) = Y(z)/X(z) \qquad (A3.16)$$

we get, for EMA

$$H(z) = \frac{\alpha}{1 - (1 - \alpha)z^{-1}} \qquad \text{(A3.17)}$$

Restricting z in the complex plane to exp(iω) on the unit circle(i.e. r = 1), the frequency response function H(ω) is given by

$$H(\omega) = \frac{\alpha}{1 - (1 - \alpha)\exp(-i\omega)} \qquad \text{(A3.18)}$$

The magnitude of H(ω) is given by (Lyons 1997)

$$|H(\omega)| = \frac{\alpha}{[1 - 2(1 - \alpha)\cos\omega + (1 - \alpha)^2]^{1/2}} \qquad \text{(A3.19)}$$

The phase is given by

$$\phi(\omega) = \tan^{-1}\left[\frac{-(1 - \alpha)\sin\omega}{1 - (1 - \alpha)\cos\omega}\right] \qquad \text{(A3.20)}$$

The amplitude and phase of H(ω) of EMA are plotted in Figs. A3.4(a) and (b) for M = 3 and M = 6. It should be noted that the phase lag is, in general, much smaller than that of the N point moving average, which makes it more popular among traders.

Rather than using Eq(A3.13) to calculate EMA, there is a different method which makes its calculation more convenient sometimes. Iterating the previously processed y value in Eq(A3.13), we can write y(n) as

$$y(n) = \sum_{k=0}^{\infty} \alpha(1 - \alpha)^k x(n - k) \qquad \text{(A3.21)}$$

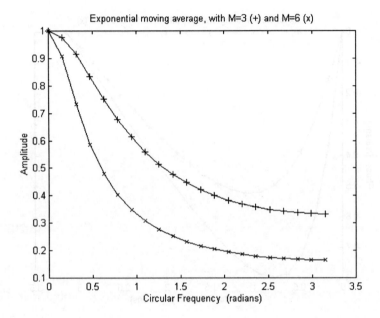

Fig. A3.4(a). Amplitude response of an exponential moving average with M = 3 (marked as +) and M = 6 (marked as x).

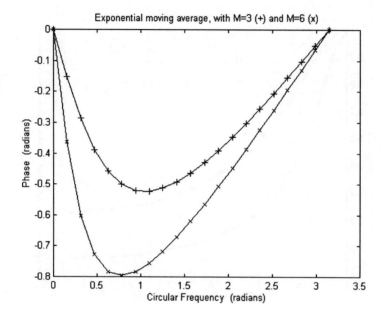

Fig. A3.4(b). Phase response of an exponential moving average with M = 3 (marked as +) and M = 6 (marked as x).

This is a causal IIR with

$$h(k) = \alpha(1-\alpha)^k \qquad\qquad\qquad (A3.22)$$

With $\alpha = 2/(M+1)$, $h(k)$ converges to zero rather quickly as k increases If M is taken to be 3, α will be equal to 0.5. Summing k from 0 to 13 will yield a rather accurate estimate of the EMA.

Appendix 4

High Pass Filters

High pass filter removes low frequency components of a signal and allows high frequency components to pass. It is thus very useful for tracking market turns, which are actually high frequency components.

Before we talk about high pass filter, we would first discuss derivative, which is a significant concept in Calculus, and can also be considered as a high pass filter.

A4.1 Derivative

Derivative can be considered as the slope of a function or signal.. Let the discrete input signal be

$$x(n) = \sin(\omega n) \tag{A4.1}$$

where n is an integer.

The derivative of the signal is

$$\frac{d}{dn} x(n) = \omega \cos(\omega n) \tag{A4.2}$$

In taking derivative, n should have been a continuous variable. Here, we try to get around the problem by considering it first to be a continuous variable and then returning it back to be an integer after taking the derivative.

Figure A4.1 plots x(n) and (d/dn)x(n) with ω = π/4. The derivative leads the input signal by π/2 radians or 90 degrees. It should be noted that the derivative is zero where the input data has its peaks and valleys. Furthermore, peak occurs when the derivative goes from positive to negative, and valley occurs when the derivative goes from negative to positive. In this book, as n represents time, we will call the derivative or first derivative the velocity operator or indicator.

Taking the derivative of Eq (A4.2) or the second derivative of Eq (A4.1), we get

$$\frac{d^2}{dn^2} x(n) = -\omega^2 \sin(\omega n) \tag{A4.3}$$

which is plotted in Fig. A4.2, together with x(n) and (d/dn)x(n). The second derivative represents the concavity of a signal. If the signal is concave down, then the second derivative is negative. If the signal is concave up, then the second derivative is positive. So, at the peak of the signal, the derivative is zero and the second derivative is negative. At the valley of the signal, the derivative is zero and the second derivative is positive. Thus, the second derivative provides a second method to differentiate whether the signal is a peak or a valley. In this book, we will call the second derivative the acceleration operator or indicator.

But how do we take the derivative of a real signal ? In many analog and digital systems, Finite Impulse Response (FIR) differentiators can be designed (Proakis and Manolakis 1996). Let us take a look at a more general signal

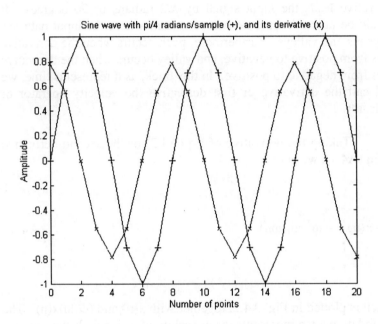

Fig. A4.1. A sine wave of circular frequency of $\pi/4$ radian (marked as +), and its (first) derivative (marked as x).

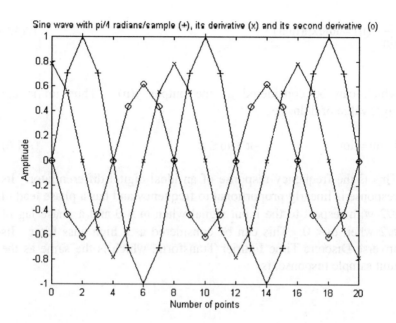

Fig. A4.2. A sine wave of circular frequency of π/4 radian (marked as +), its (first) derivative (marked as x) and its second derivative (marked as 0).

$x(n) = \exp(i\omega n) = \cos(\omega n) + i\sin(\omega n)$ (A4.4)

Taking derivative of Eq (A4.4) yields

$$\frac{d}{dn}x(n) = i\omega \exp(i\omega n)$$ (A4.5)

which can be considered as the output y(n). Thus $i\omega$ is the eigenvalue of d/dn. i.e.

$H(\omega) = i\omega$ $-\pi \leq \omega \leq \pi$ (A4.6)

This is the frequency response of an ideal digital differentiator. Its response is linearly proportional to frequency and has a phase lead of $\pi/2$ with respect to the input signal when $\omega > 0$ and a phase lag of $\pi/2$ when $\omega < 0$. This can be considered as a high pass filter. Its Inverse Discrete Time Fourier Transform, which is the same as the unit sample response, is

$$h(k) = \frac{1}{2\pi}\int_{-\pi}^{\pi} H(\omega)\, e^{i\omega k}\, d\omega = \frac{\cos \pi k}{k} \qquad -\infty < k < \infty, k \neq 0$$

(A4.7)

This example is mentioned to show how an ideal differentiator should look like. However, this is a non-causal filter and cannot be applied in trading, where future data is not available. Causal filters will be considered below.

A4.2 Moving Difference

This high pass (causal) filter is a twin or mirror filter of the two point moving average low pass filter discussed in Appendix 3. Its output is defined as (Strang and Nguyen 1997)

$$y(n) = (1/2)x(n) - (1/2)x(n-1) \tag{A4.8}$$

(This definition of moving difference is essentially the same as momentum defined by technical analysts (see Eq 4.5), except that it has a normalization constant ½.)

The frequency response function $H(\omega)$, which is the Discrete Time Fourier Transform (DTFT) of h, is given by

$$H(\omega) = (1/2) - (1/2)\exp(-i\omega) = \sin(\omega/2)\, i\exp(-i\omega/2) \tag{A4.9}$$

Its magnitude is

$$|H(\omega)| = |\sin(\omega/2)| \tag{A4.10}$$

and its phase is

$$\phi(\omega) = \begin{cases} \dfrac{\pi}{2} - \dfrac{\omega}{2} & 0 < \omega \le \pi \\ -\dfrac{\pi}{2} - \dfrac{\omega}{2} & -\pi \le \omega < 0 \end{cases} \tag{A4.11}$$

$|H(\omega)|$ and $\phi(\omega)$ are plotted in Figs. A4.3(a) and (b). This two point moving difference has a phase lag of $\omega/2$ from the ideal case of $\pi/2$ phase lead for $\omega > 0$ or $\pi/2$ phase lag for $\omega < 0$. This would be more or less equivalent to a lag of half a time unit. For example, if a trader is trading in a 30-minute time chart, he or she would not realize a

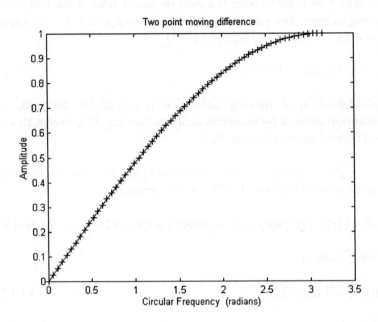

Fig. A4.3(a). Amplitude response of a two point moving difference.

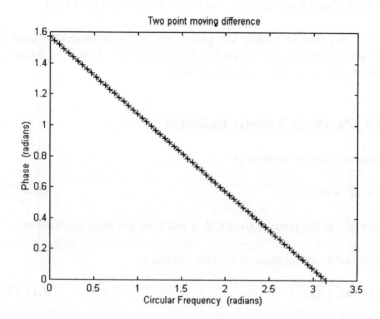

Fig. A4.3(b). Phase response of a two point moving difference.

turning point until about 15 minutes later, causing excessive delay in buy-sell decision, which would translate to lost profits. Figure A4.4 plots a sine wave with $\pi/4$ radian per sample as well as the signal after being filtered by a two point moving difference. Note that there is a $\pi/8$ radian phase lag from the ideal case of $\pi/2$ phase lead.

In order to reduce the phase lag, we will introduce here a new moving difference which has less phase lag. It will be called a parabolic velocity operator or indicator.

A4.3 Parabolic Velocity Indicator

A parabola can be written as

$$x(t) = dt^2 + et + f \qquad\qquad (A4.12)$$

where $x(t)$ is the price at time t; d, e and f are constant coefficients.

For discrete-time signals, it will be written as

$$x(n) = dn^2 + en + f \qquad\qquad (A4.13)$$

We are interested to find the derivative of the parabola at $n = 0$, which is the most recent data point. We write

$$x_0 = x(0) = f \qquad\qquad (A4.14a)$$

$$x_{-1} = x(-1) = d - e + f \qquad\qquad (A4.14b)$$

$$x_{-2} = x(-2) = 4d - 2e + f \qquad\qquad (A4.14c)$$

Solving Eq (A4.14a – c) for d, e and f, we get

$$d = (1/2)x_0 - x_{-1} + (1/2)x_{-2} \qquad\qquad (A4.15a)$$

$$e = (3/2)x_0 - 2x_{-1} + (1/2)x_{-2} \qquad\qquad (A4.15b)$$

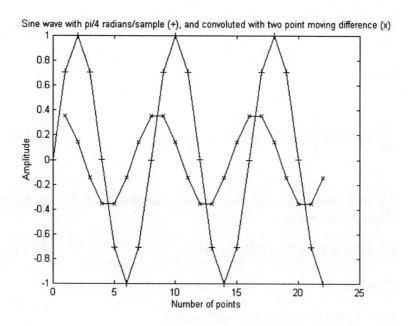

Fig. A4.4. A sine wave of circular frequency of $\pi/4$ radian (marked as +), and convoluted (or filtered) with a two point moving difference (marked as x).

$$f = x_0 \tag{A4.15c}$$

Taking the derivative of Eq (A4.13), we arrive at

$$\frac{dx}{dn} = 2dn + e \tag{A4.16}$$

At $n = 0$,

$$\frac{dx}{dn}\Big|_{n=0} = e = \frac{3}{2}x_0 - 2x_{-1} + \frac{1}{2}x_{-2} \tag{A4.17}$$

We will thus define the unit sample response h of the parabolic velocity indicator as

$$h = (h(0), h(1), h(2)) = (3/2, -2, \frac{1}{2}) \tag{A4.18}$$

Therefore, the output response is given by the convolution sum

$$y(n) = h(0)x(n) + h(1)x(n-1) + h(2)x(n-2)$$

$$= (3/2)x(n) - 2x(n-1) + (1/2)x(n-2) \tag{A4.19}$$

The frequency response or DTFT of h is given by

$$H(\omega) = (3/2) - 2\exp(-i\omega) + (1/2)\exp(-2i\omega)$$

$$= (3/2) - 2\cos(\omega) + (1/2)\cos(2\omega) + i[2\sin(\omega) - (1/2)\sin(2\omega)]$$

$$\tag{A4.20}$$

The magnitude and phase of $H(\omega)$ are

$$|H(\omega)|$$

$$= \{[(3/2) - 2\cos(\omega) + (1/2)\cos(2\omega)]^2 + [2\sin(\omega) - (1/2)\sin(2\omega)]^2\}^{1/2}$$

$$\text{(A4.21)}$$

$$\phi(\omega) = \tan^{-1}\left(\frac{2\sin\omega - (1/2)\sin 2\omega}{3/2 - 2\cos\omega + (1/2)\cos 2\omega}\right) \qquad \text{(A4.22)}$$

$|H(\omega)|$ and $\phi(\omega)$ are plotted in Figs. A4.5(a) and (b). From the plot of $\phi(\omega)$, we can see that, comparing to the phase of the two point moving difference in Fig. A4.3(b), it has a much less phase lag from the ideal case of $\pi/2$ phase lead.

When the output response of the parabolic velocity indicator is approximately zero, another indicator, the parabolic acceleration indicator can help to determine whether the price is at its peak or at its valley. We will introduce this new indicator in the next section.

A4.4 Parabolic Acceleration Indicator

Taking the second derivative of Eq(A4.13) or the derivative of Eq (A4.16), we get

$$\frac{d^2x}{dn^2} = 2d = x_0 - 2x_{-1} + x_{-2} \qquad \text{(A4.23)}$$

As d^2x/dn^2 is independent of n, acceleration is the same for n = 0, –1, –2.

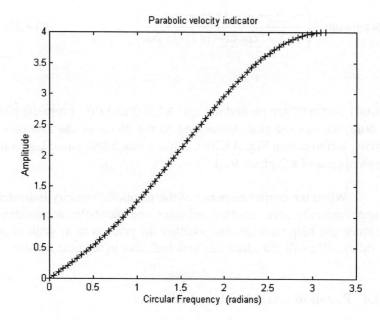

Fig. A4.5(a). Amplitude response of a parabolic velocity indicator.

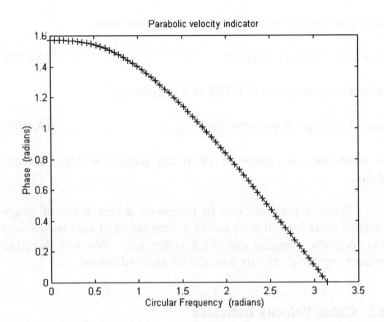

Fig. A4.5(b). Phase response of a parabolic velocity indicator.

We will define the unit sample response h of the parabolic acceleration indicator as

$$h = (h(0), h(1), h(2)) = (1, -2, 1) \qquad (A4.24)$$

The output response is given by the convolution sum

$$y(n) = x(n) - 2x(n-1) + x(n-2) \qquad (A4.25)$$

The frequency response or DTFT of h is given by

$$H(\omega) = 1 - 2\exp(-i\omega) + \exp(-2i\omega) \qquad (A4.26)$$

The amplitude and phase of $H(\omega)$ are plotted in Figs. A4.6(a) and (b).

While a parabola can fit piecewise a sine wave of single frequency quite well, it does not fit a summation of sine waves very well. A cubic function can do a better job. We will therefore introduce the cubic velocity and acceleration indicators.

A4.5 Cubic Velocity Indicator

A cubic function can be written as

$$x(t) = ct^3 + dt^2 + et + f \qquad (A4.27)$$

where c, d, e and f are constant coefficients. When c = 0, Eq (A4.27) reduces to that of a parabola. For discrete time signals, Eq (A4.27) will be written as

$$x(n) = cn^3 + dn^2 + en + f \qquad (A4.28)$$

We are interested to find the derivative of the cubic function at n = 0, which is the most recent data point.

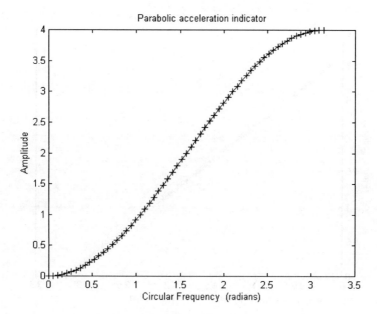

Fig. A4.6(a). Amplitude response of a parabolic acceleration indicator.

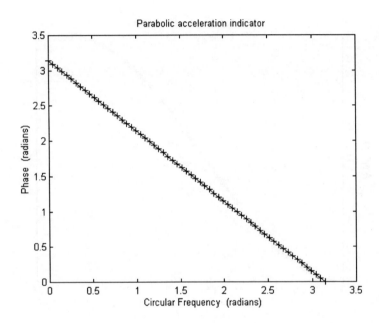

Fig. A4.6(b). Phase response of a parabolic acceleration indicator.

We write

$$x_0 = x(0) = f \tag{A4.29a}$$

$$x_{-1} = x(-1) = -c + d - e + f \tag{A4.29b}$$

$$x_{-2} = x(-2) = -8c + 4d - 2e + f \tag{A4.29c}$$

$$x_{-3} = x(-3) = -27c + 9d - 3e + f \tag{A4.29d}$$

Solving Eq (A4.29a–d) for c, d, e and f, we get

$$c = (x_0 - 3x_{-1} + 3x_{-2} - x_{-3})/6 \tag{A4.30a}$$

$$d = (2x_0 - 5x_{-1} + 4x_{-2} - x_{-3})/2 \tag{A4.30b}$$

$$e = (11x_0 - 18x_{-1} + 9x_{-2} - 2x_{-3})/6 \tag{A4.30c}$$

$$f = x_0 \tag{A4.30d}$$

Taking the derivative of Eq (A4.28), we arrive at

$$\frac{dx}{dn} = 3cn^2 + 2dn + e \tag{A4.31}$$

At n = 0,

$$\frac{dx}{dn}\bigg|_{n=0} = e = (11x_0 - 18x_{-1} + 9x_{-2} - 2x_{-3})/6 \tag{A4.32}$$

We will define the unit sample response h of the cubic velocity indicator as h = (h(0), h(1), h(2), h(3)) = (11/6, −3, 3/2, −1/3)   (A4.33)

Thus, the output response is given by the convolution sum

y(n) = (11/6)x(n) − 3x(n−1) + (3/2)x(n−2) − (1/3)x(n−3)   (A4.34)

The frequency response or DTFT of h is given by

H(ω) = (11/6) − 3exp(−iω) + (3/2)exp(−2iω) − (1/3)exp(−3iω)

(A4.35)

The amplitude and phase of H(ω) are plotted in Figs. A4.7(a) and (b). Comparing to the phase of the parabolic velocity indicator in Fig. A4.5(b), the phase of the cubic velocity indicator in Fig. A4.7(b) has even less phase lag from the ideal case of $\pi/2$ phase lead.

A4.6 Cubic Acceleration Indicator

Taking the second derivative of Eq (A4.28) or the derivative of Eq (A4.31), we get

$$\frac{d^2x}{dn^2} = 6cn + 2d$$ (A4.36)

At n = 0,

$$\frac{d^2x}{dn^2}\bigg|_{n=0} = 2d = 2x_0 - 5x_{-1} + 4x_{-2} - x_{-3}$$ (A4.37)

We will define the unit sample response h of the cubic acceleration indicator as

h = (h(0), h(1), h(2), h(3)) = (2, −5, 4, −1)   (A4.38)

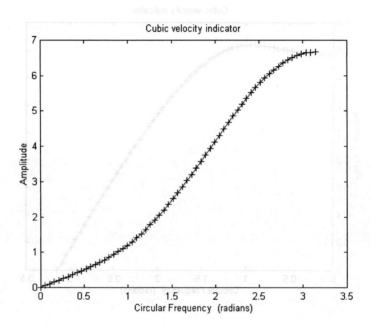

Fig. A4.7(a). Amplitude response of a cubic velocity indicator.

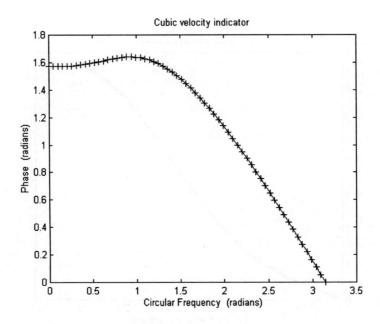

Fig. A4.7(b). Phase response of a cubic velocity indicator.

The output response is given by the convolution sum

$$y(n) = 2x(n) - 5x(n-1) + 4x(n-2) - x(n-3) \qquad (A4.39)$$

The frequency response or DTFT of h is given by

$$H(\omega) = 2 - 5\exp(-i\omega) + 4\exp(-2i\omega) - \exp(-3i\omega) \qquad (A4.40)$$

The amplitude and phase of $H(\omega)$ are plotted in Figs. A4.8(a) and (b). Comparing to the phase of the parabolic acceleration indicator in Fig. A4.6(b), the phase of the cubic acceleration indicator in Fig. A4.8(b) has much less phase lag from the ideal case of π phase lead.

A4.7 Properties of a Cubic Function

We will investigate the behavior of a continuous cubic function, which is given by Eq (A4.27). We will then take a look and see whether a cubic function can fit piecewise a signal which consists of the summation of two sine waves. Taking first and second derivatives of Eq (A4.27), we get

$$\frac{dx}{dt} = 3ct^2 + 2dt + e \qquad (A4.41)$$

$$\frac{d^2x}{dt^2} = 6ct + 2d \qquad (A4.42)$$

Equating Eq (A4.42) to zero, we get

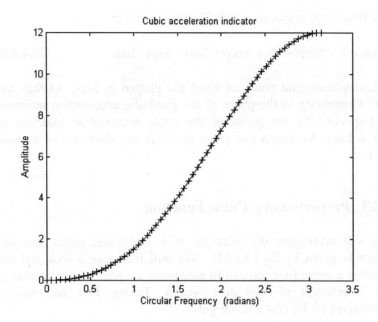

Fig. A4.8(a). Amplitude response of a cubic acceleration indicator.

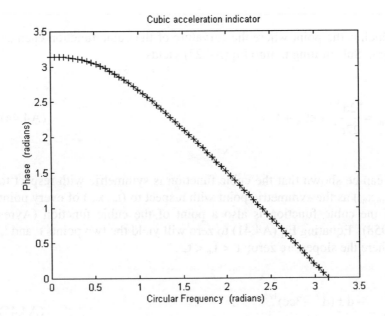

Fig. A4.8(b). Phase response of a cubic acceleration indicator.

$$t_m = -\frac{d}{3c} \qquad\qquad (A4.43)$$

which is the point where the curvature of the cubic function changes sign. Substituting t_m into Eq (A4.27) yields

$$x_m = \frac{2d^3}{27c^3} + et_m + f \qquad\qquad (A4.44)$$

It can be shown that the cubic function is symmetric with respect to (t_m, x_m) as the symmetric point with respect to (t_m, x_m) of every point of the cubic function is also a point of the cubic function (Ayres 1958). Equating Eq (A4.41) to zero will yield the two points t_- and t_+ where the slopes are zero; $t_- < t_m < t_+$.

$$t_\pm = \frac{-d \pm (d^2 - 3ce)^{1/2}}{3c} \qquad\qquad (A4.45)$$

Substituting Eq (A4.45) into Eq (A4.27) yields

$$x_\pm = x_m \mp \frac{2(d^2 - 3ce)^{3/2}}{27c^2} \qquad\qquad (A4.46)$$

It can be shown that, for Eqs (A4.45) and (A4.46), when c > 0, the positive square root of ($d^2 - 3ce$) should be taken, while when c < 0, the negative square root of (d^2-3ce) should be taken.

Can a cubic function simulate summation of sine waves piecemeal and pinpoint its turning points? A plot of the summation of two sine waves, one with amplitude of 1.0 and circular frequency of $\pi/4$ radian and the other with amplitude of 2.0 and circular frequency of $\pi/16$ radian is given in Fig. A4.9. Four of the points (marked as o) were provided for fitting to a cubic function. The two turning points were calculated and plotted (marked as x). It can be seen that the calculated points correspond to the actual turning points quite well. This provides some evidence that for a summation of two sine waves, a fitted cubic function can forecast the turning points quite well if the four points used for fitting are not too far from the turning points. This property will be employed when we introduce the cubic vertex indicator in the next appendix.

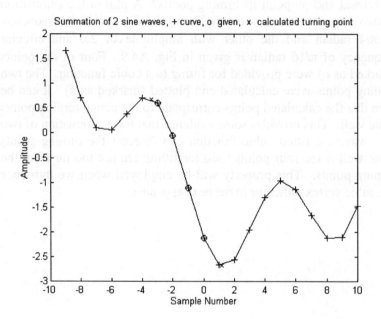

Fig. A4.9. Summation of two sine waves (marked as +). Four of the points (marked as 0) were used to fit a cubic function, which was then used to calculate two turning points (marked as x).

Appendix 5

Vertices

The parabolic and cubic vertex indicators will be derived here.

A5.1 Parabolic Vertex Indicator

A parabola can be written as

$$x(t) = dt^2 + et + f \qquad (A5.1)$$

It can also be written as

$$(t - t_v)^2 = 2p(x - x_v) \qquad (A5.2)$$

where (t_v, x_v) is the vertex (or turning point) of the parabola and $p/2$ is the distance from the focus of the parabola to the vertex (Protter and Morrey 1963).

Eq (A5.1) can be rewritten in the form of Eq (A5.2), yielding

$$t_v = -\frac{e}{2d} \qquad (A5.3)$$

An alternative method to find t_v is to equate the derivative of $x(t)$ in Eq (A5.1), i.e., dx/dt to zero. At that point, $t = t_v$, and Eq

191

(A5.3) can be deduced. If d = 0, Eq (A5.1) reduces to the equation of a straight line. In that case, no turning point exists. If the present time (of the market) is taken to be t = 0, t_v shows how far in time the market is away from the turning point. When $t_v = 0$, the market is exactly at the turning point.

Substituting Eq (A4.15) into Eq (A5.3) yields the number of bars the turning point is from the present time, which is taken to be t = 0 or n = 0.

$$t_v(0) = \frac{-\left[\frac{3}{2}x(0) - 2x(-1) + \frac{1}{2}x(-2)\right]}{x(0) - 2x(-1) + x(-2)} \tag{A5.4}$$

The number of bars the turning point is from the nth bar is

$$t_v(n) = \frac{-\left[\frac{3}{2}x(n) - 2x(n-1) + \frac{1}{2}x(n-2)\right]}{x(n) - 2x(n-1) + x(n-2)} \tag{A5.5}$$

where x is the closing price or the smoothed closing price.

A5.2 Cubic Vertex Indicator

A cubic function can be written as

$$x(t) = ct^3 + dt^2 + et + f \qquad (A5.6)$$

Equating the derivative of x(t) to zero yields the two turning points of the cubic function

$$t_\pm(n) = \frac{-d \pm \sqrt{d^2 - 3ce}}{3c} \qquad (A5.7)$$

where, from Eq (A4.30),

$$c = [x(n)-3x(n-1)+3x(n-2)-x(n-3]/6 \neq 0 \qquad (A5.8)$$

$$d = [2x(n)-5x(n-1)+4x(n-2)-x(n-3)]/2 \qquad (A5.9)$$

$$e = [11x(n)-18x(n-1)+9x(n-2)-2x(n-3)]/6 \qquad (A5.10)$$

and x is the closing or the smoothed closing price.

It should be noted that the d in Eq(A5.9) and e in Eq(A5.10) are different from the d and e in Eq(A5.3) as the former are derived by fitting market price data to a cubic function using four points, while the latter are derived by fitting market price data to a parabola using three points.

When c = 0, the cubic function reduces to that of a parabola, which has only one turning point. The timing of the turning point will be given by $-e/(2d)$ where d and e are given by Eq(A5.9) and Eq (A5.10) respectively.

Appendix 6

Downsampling and Upsampling

Traders work in different timeframes, e.g. 15-minutes chart, 60-minutes chart, etc . A 15-minutes chart can be reduced to a 60-minutes chart. This involves a concept called downsampling. Downsampling is significant as it transforms the frequency content of a signal.

Before we discuss the concept of downsampling, we will introduce two other concepts, the delay operator and the advance operator.

The shift or delay operator, S, is a linear operator and can be represented by a matrix (Strang and Nguyen 1997). It is a causal operator and can be written as a lower triangular matrix :

$$Sx = \begin{bmatrix} \cdot & \cdot & \cdot & \cdot & \cdot & \cdot \\ \cdot & 0 & 0 & 0 & 0 & \cdot \\ \cdot & 1 & 0 & 0 & 0 & \cdot \\ \cdot & 0 & 1 & 0 & 0 & \cdot \\ \cdot & 0 & 0 & 1 & 0 & \cdot \\ \cdot & \cdot & \cdot & \cdot & \cdot & \cdot \end{bmatrix} \begin{bmatrix} \cdot \\ x(-1) \\ x(0) \\ x(1) \\ x(2) \\ \cdot \end{bmatrix} = \begin{bmatrix} \cdot \\ x(-2) \\ x(-1) \\ x(0) \\ x(1) \\ \cdot \end{bmatrix} = \begin{bmatrix} \cdot \\ y(-1) \\ y(0) \\ y(1) \\ y(2) \\ \cdot \end{bmatrix} = y \quad (A6.1)$$

where **x** is the input and **y** is the output.

We can also simply write

$$y(n) = x(n-1) \tag{A6.2}$$

This is similar to the situation where time is continuous. A graph of f(t), when shifted one unit time to the right, becomes the graph of f(t-1). The delayed function $f_d(t)$, can be written as

$$f_d(t) = f(t-1) \tag{A6.3}$$

At t = 1, the delayed function equals the original function at t = 0.

The advance operator or **S** inverse, S^{-1}, has an effect opposite to **S**. It can be written as an upper triangular matrix:

$$S^{-1}x = \begin{bmatrix} . & . & . & . & . & . \\ . & 0 & 1 & 0 & 0 & . \\ . & 0 & 0 & 1 & 0 & . \\ . & 0 & 0 & 0 & 1 & . \\ . & 0 & 0 & 0 & 0 & . \\ . & . & . & . & . & . \end{bmatrix} \begin{bmatrix} . \\ x(-1) \\ x(0) \\ x(1) \\ x(2) \\ . \end{bmatrix} = \begin{bmatrix} . \\ x(0) \\ x(1) \\ x(2) \\ x(3) \\ . \end{bmatrix} = \begin{bmatrix} . \\ y(-1) \\ y(0) \\ y(1) \\ y(2) \\ . \end{bmatrix} = y \tag{A6.4}$$

Thus,

$$y(n) = x(n + 1) \tag{A6.5}$$

It can be shown that

$$S^{-1}S\,x = SS^{-1}\,x = x \qquad\qquad (A6.6)$$

or, more generally

$$S^{-n}S^n\,x = S^nS^{-n}\,x = x \qquad\qquad (A6.7)$$

As we discussed in Appendix 2, the Discrete Time Fourier Transform of the unit sample response, **H**, is shift-invariant. This property can be written as

$$H(Sx) = S(Hx) \qquad\qquad (A6.8)$$

A shift of the input causes a shift of the output.

As each column of **H** is a delay of the previous column, and all elements of the nth diagonal equals $h(n)$, we can write

$$H = \Sigma\, h(n)\, S^n \qquad\qquad (A6.9)$$

A6.1 Downsampling

The sequence $v(n) = x(Mn)$ is formed by taking every M^{th} sample of $x(n)$. This operation is called downsampling or decimation (Hayes 1999, Strang and Nguyen 1997).

When every other component is removed, downsampling is represented by the symbol ($\downarrow 2$) (pronounced "down two"), which can be written as a matrix. When odd-numbered components are removed, the matrix form of downsampling is

$$(\downarrow 2)x = \begin{bmatrix} . & . & . & . & . & . & . \\ . & 1 & 0 & 0 & 0 & 0 & . \\ . & 0 & 0 & 1 & 0 & 0 & . \\ . & . & . & 0 & 0 & 1 & . \\ . & . & . & . & . & . & . \end{bmatrix} \begin{bmatrix} . \\ x(-2) \\ x(-1) \\ x(0) \\ x(1) \\ x(2) \\ . \end{bmatrix} = \begin{bmatrix} . \\ x(-2) \\ x(0) \\ x(2) \\ . \end{bmatrix} = \begin{bmatrix} . \\ v(-1) \\ v(0) \\ v(1) \\ . \end{bmatrix} = v$$

(A6.10)

The nth component of $\mathbf{v} = (\downarrow 2)\mathbf{x}$ is the $(2n)^{th}$ component of x, i.e.,

$$v(n) = x(2n) \qquad\qquad (A6.11)$$

This downsampling matrix is, thus, the identity matrix, **I**, with odd-numbered rows removed. The identity matrix is a matrix with diagonal elements being 1 and all other elements 0.

In stock market charts, $(\downarrow 2)$ data in the 15-minutes chart will yield the 30-minutes chart; $(\downarrow 4)$ data in the 15-minutes chart will yield the 60-minutes chart.

A6.2 Upsampling

The transpose of downsampling, $(\downarrow 2)^T$, is upsampling :

$$(\downarrow 2)^T = (\uparrow 2) \qquad\qquad (A6.12)$$

Upsampling puts zero into the odd-numbered components :

$$u(n) = \begin{cases} v(k) & \text{if } n = 2k \\ 0 & \text{if } n = 2k+1 \end{cases} \tag{A6.13}$$

The matrix form of upsampling is

$$(\uparrow 2)v = \begin{bmatrix} . & . & . & . & . \\ . & 1 & 0 & 0 & . \\ . & 0 & 0 & 0 & . \\ . & 0 & 1 & 0 & . \\ . & 0 & 0 & 0 & . \\ . & 0 & 0 & 1 & 0 \\ . & . & . & . & . \end{bmatrix} \begin{bmatrix} . \\ v(-1) \\ v(0) \\ v(1) \\ . \end{bmatrix} = \begin{bmatrix} . \\ v(-1) \\ 0 \\ v(0) \\ 0 \\ v(1) \\ . \end{bmatrix} = \begin{bmatrix} . \\ u(-2) \\ u(-1) \\ u(0) \\ u(1) \\ u(2) \\ . \end{bmatrix} = u$$

$$\tag{A6.14}$$

The upsampling matrix is the matrix with zero rows being inserted between the rows of the identity matrix.

It can be shown that

$$(\downarrow 2)(\uparrow 2) = \mathbf{I} \tag{A6.15}$$

However,

$$(\uparrow 2)(\downarrow 2) \neq \mathbf{I} \qquad \text{(A6.16)}$$

as $(\downarrow 2)$ removes the odd-numbered components and $(\uparrow 2)$ replaces the lost components by zeros. Thus,

$$(\downarrow 2)(\uparrow 2)\mathbf{x} = \mathbf{x} \qquad \text{(A6.17)}$$

But,

$$(\uparrow 2)(\downarrow 2)\mathbf{x} \neq \mathbf{x} \qquad \text{(A6.18)}$$

However, we can reconstruct $\mathbf{x}$ if we can make use of the delay and advance operators :

$$\mathbf{S}^{-1}(\uparrow 2)(\downarrow 2)\mathbf{Sx} + (\uparrow 2)(\downarrow 2)\mathbf{x} = \mathbf{x} \qquad \text{(A6.19)}$$

or, more generally,

$$\sum_{\ell=0}^{N-1} \mathbf{S}^{-\ell} (\uparrow M)(\downarrow M)\mathbf{S}^{\ell} \, \mathbf{x} = \mathbf{x} \qquad \text{(A6.20)}$$

Traders usually use the same operator or indicator in different time frames. Data from a larger time frame (e.g. 60-minutes chart) can be downsampled from a smaller time frame (e.g. 15-minutes chart). So, the question is, what are the differences in operator responses of a signal and a downsampled signal? Let us take a look at an example where the derivative operator, d/dn is used. Let the signal be x(n).

$$x(n) = \sin \frac{\pi n}{16} \qquad\qquad (A6.21)$$

$$\frac{d}{dn} x(n) = \frac{\pi}{16} \cos \frac{\pi n}{16} \qquad\qquad (A6.22)$$

$$\left[(\downarrow 4) x \right](n) = \sin \frac{\pi n}{4} \qquad\qquad (A6.23)$$

$$\left[\frac{d}{dn} (\downarrow 4) x \right](n) = \frac{\pi}{4} \cos \frac{\pi n}{4} \qquad\qquad (A6.24)$$

Comparing Eq (A6.24) with Eq (A6.22), we can see that the amplitude of the response of the derivative operator is larger by a factor of 4 in the ($\downarrow$4) timeframe than that of the original timeframe. In trading, while amplitude plays a role in the traders' decision making, phase (or time) shift plays a more significant role. We will take a look and see how the phase is shifted in the ($\downarrow$4) timeframe from that of the original timeframe. The ($\downarrow$4) timeframe should, ordinarily, have only a quarter of the number of data points of the original timeframe. The initial point where we start downsampling would determine what phases of the signal we would be seeing. If we would like to see the various phases of the downsampled signal, we would downsample the original signal starting at different adjacent initial points, operate on the downsampled signals and then reconstruct them back as one signal by using upsampling. This process will be represented by the following equation.

$$[Dx](n) = \left[\sum_{\ell=0}^{3} d_{\ell} x\right](n) = \left[\sum_{\ell=0}^{3} S^{-\ell} (\uparrow 4)\frac{d}{dn}(\downarrow 4)S^{\ell}x\right](n)$$

$$= \frac{\pi}{4}\cos\frac{\pi}{16}n = 4\frac{d}{dn}x(n) \qquad (A6.25)$$

where

$$d_{\ell} = S^{-\ell} (\uparrow 4)\frac{d}{dn}(\downarrow 4)S^{\ell} \qquad (A6.26)$$

Figure A6.1(a) shows the input signal $x(n)$, with derivative of $x(n)$, i.e., $(d/dn)x(n)$, plotted in Fig. A6.1(b) and $[Dx](n)$ plotted in a reconstructed ($\downarrow 4$) timeframe in Fig. A6.1(c). It should be noted that in an ordinary ($\downarrow 4$) timeframe, traders see only every other four points in Fig. A6.1(c), i.e. $[d_{\ell}x](n)$ where $\ell = 0, 1, 2, 3$. Only when $\ell = 0$ will there be no phase shift with respect to the original timeframe as shown in Fig. A6.1(b). When $\ell = 1, 2, 3$, the output response of the

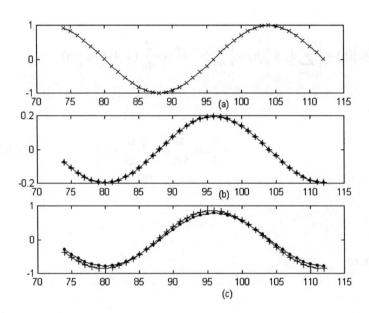

Fig. A6.1(a) A sine wave of circular frequency of $\pi/16$ radian (marked as x); (b) the sine wave is filtered with a cubic velocity indicator (marked as +), and compared with its derivative (marked as); (c) the sine wave is downsampled four (i.e. every fourth point is taken), the downsampled signal is filtered with a cubic velocity indicator (marked as +) and compared with its derivative (marked as .). The initial point where downsampling starts is shifted and the calculation repeated.

operator in the ($\downarrow$4) timeframe has a phase lag with respect to that in the original timeframe of Fig. A6.1(b). In this particular case, the phase lag is not caused by the derivative operator, but caused by the signal being downsampled. The output signal of the derivative operator leads the input signal by $\pi/2$, which is independent of the frequency of the input signal. However, other operators or indicators, e.g., the cubic velocity indicator is a function of frequency of the input signal. The output signal was compared in Fig. A6.1(b) and Fig. A6.1(c) to the output response of the cubic velocity indicator, which is slightly dependent on frequency. In Fig. A6.1(b), the output response of the cubic velocity indicator almost exactly overlap with results calculated from the derivative, illustrating that the indicator can simulate the derivative quite well for a frequency of $\pi/16$ radians. In the reconstructed ($\downarrow$4) timeframe of Fig. A6.1(c), the response of the cubic velocity indicator operated on a frequency of the $\pi/4$ radians has a slight phase lead compared to the derivative. This is consistent with the phase plot of the cubic velocity indicator shown in Fig. A4.7(b).

In the example above, downsampling transforms a single frequency signal to another single frequency signal of the same shape. This may not necessarily be the case, as we will show in the next section.

A6.3 Downsampling in the Frequency Domain

Downsampling a pure exponential signal, $x(n) = \exp(in\omega)$, is quite straightforward. For example, the nth component of $\mathbf{v} = (\downarrow 2)\mathbf{x}$ is

$$v(n) = \exp(i2n\omega) = x(2n) \tag{A6.27}$$

which is a pure exponential with frequency 2ω.

The Fourier Transform of Eq(A6.27) should be

$$V(2\omega) = X(\omega) \tag{A6.28}$$

or

$$V(\omega) = X(\omega/2) \tag{A6.29}$$

However, this is not correct.

If x_0 is another pure exponential, with frequency $\omega + \pi$, then

$$x_0(n) = \exp[in(\omega + \pi)] \tag{A6.30}$$

The nth component of $v_0 = (\downarrow 2)x_0$ is

$$v_0(n) = \exp[i2n(\omega + \pi)] = \exp(i2n\omega) \tag{A6.31}$$

which is the same as $v(n)$. Thus $(\downarrow 2)$ yields a frequency 2ω by doubling ω, and also by doubling $\omega + \pi$. The Fourier Transform of $v = (\downarrow 2)x$ should be (Strang and Nguyen 1997)

$$V(\omega) = \frac{1}{2}\left[X\left(\frac{\omega}{2}\right) + X\left(\frac{\omega}{2} + \pi\right)\right] \tag{A6.32}$$

This can be extended to $(\downarrow M)$. The nth component of $v = (\downarrow M)x$ is

$$v(n) = x(Mn) \tag{A6-33}$$

whose Fourier Transform is (Strang and Nguyen 1997)

$$V(\omega) = \frac{1}{M}\left[X\left(\frac{\omega}{M}\right) + X\left(\frac{\omega + 2\pi}{M}\right) + \dots + X\left(\frac{\omega + (M-1)2\pi}{M}\right)\right]$$

(A6.34)

Thus, there are M-1 aliases in downsampling. Given a sequence x(n), ambiguity exists as to what frequency or mixture of frequencies the original signal contains. This problem can be solved by eliminating the high frequency components from the original signal by applying a low pass filter. Downsampling is then performed on the filtered signal.

Appendix 7

Wavelets

Wavelet analysis can be considered as an extension of Fourier Analysis. We will first take a look at Fourier Analysis.

A7.1 Fourier Analysis

A periodic function $f(t)$ with period T_0 can be represented as a sum of sines and cosines, which is called a Fourier series given by the expression (Brigham 1974, p75).

$$f(t) = \frac{a_0}{2} + \sum_{n=1}^{\infty} [a_n \cos(2\pi n f_0 t) + b_n \sin(2\pi n f_0 t)] \qquad (A7.1)$$

where f_0 is the fundamental frequency and is equal to $1/T_0$. The coefficients are given by the integrals

$$a_n = \frac{2}{T_0} \int_{-T_0/2}^{T_0/2} f(t) \cos(2\pi n f_0 t) dt \qquad n = 0,1,2,3,... \qquad (A7.2)$$

$$b_n = \frac{2}{T_0} \int_{-T_0/2}^{T_0/2} f(t)\sin(2\pi n f_0 t)dt \qquad n = 1,2,3,... \qquad (A7.3)$$

Eq (A7.1) can be expressed as sine waves only, with phases, θ_n.

$$f(t) = \frac{a_0}{2} + \sum_{n=1}^{\infty} c_n \sin(2\pi n f_0 t + \theta_n) \qquad (A7.4)$$

where

$$c_n = \sqrt{a_n^2 + b_n^2} \qquad n = 1,2,3,... \qquad (A7.5)$$

$$\theta_n = \tan^{-1}\left(\frac{a_n}{b_n}\right) \qquad n = 1,2,3,... \qquad (A7.6)$$

If the function f(t) is not periodic, we can assume that it is periodic with period T_0 equals to the whole sampling time interval. If we know c_n and θ_n, we can plot out each individual sine wave and observe which direction each one is heading.

However, Fourier Analysis has its limitation. Its building blocks are sines and cosines, which oscillate for all time. Therefore, it does not work well with signals of short duration. For example, the Fourier Analysis of a pulse-like signal will yield a large number of waves with high frequency — each of very long duration. When they are added together, they cancel one another out except at the point when they strengthen one another to produce the pulse. Thus, a Fourier Transform cannot give us information about time. Furthermore, it is also highly susceptible to errors. If there is a mistake in the last few minutes of an one-hour signal, the mistake will corrupt the whole Fourier Transform (Hubbard 1998, p23), as the information in one part of a signal is spread throughout the whole transform.

Fourier Analysis requires us to choose between time or frequency. But quite often, we would like to know both time and frequency rather accurately. Windowed Fourier Transform solves some of the problems. Each window corresponds to a specific interval of time, and the frequencies of the signal within that window is analyzed. As each window has a fixed finite length, it imposes quite some drawback. The smaller the window, the more accurate a sharp pulse can be located, but the lower frequency components in the signal will not be observed. If a bigger window is chosen, more of the low frequencies can be seen, but at the sacrifice of locating an event in time.

A7.2 Wavelet Analysis

A new mathematical technique, called wavelet analysis, can resolve the above-mentioned difficulty. It uses local basis functions called wavelets that can be stretched and translated, thus allowing a flexible resolution in both frequency and time. The window narrows when high frequency signals need to be focused and widens when low frequency signals need to be searched (Lau and Weng 1995).

One of the best known wavelet system is that formed by the sinc function which is written as

$$\phi(t) = \text{sinc}(\pi t) = [\sin(\pi t)]/(\pi t) \tag{A7.7}$$

Its Fourier Transform, i.e., its representation in the frequency domain, is a rectangular function and is thus confined to a finite duration, i.e., supported compactly.

Fourier Transform is defined as (Brigham 1974)

$$\Phi(f) = \int_{-\infty}^{\infty} \phi(t) \exp(-i2\pi ft) dt \tag{A7.8}$$

or

$$\Phi(\omega) = \int_{-\infty}^{\infty} \phi(t) \exp(-i\omega t) dt \tag{A7.9}$$

while inverse Fourier Transform is defined as

$$\phi(t) = \int_{-\infty}^{\infty} \Phi(f) \exp(i2\pi ft) df \tag{A7.10}$$

or

$$\phi(t) = \frac{1}{2\pi} \int_{-\infty}^{\infty} \Phi(\omega) \exp(i\omega t) d\omega \tag{A7.11}$$

The Fourier Transform of the sinc function is given by (Rao and Bopardikar 1998, p72)

$$\Phi(\omega) = \int_{-\infty}^{\infty} \frac{\sin \pi t}{\pi t} \exp(-i\omega t) dt = \begin{cases} 1 & |\omega| \le \pi \\ 0 & \text{otherwise} \end{cases} \tag{A7.12}$$

and is thus bandlimited to the frequency range $-\pi \leq \omega \leq \pi$.

In order to qualify as a scaling function, which is the father of wavelets (Hubbard 1998), $\phi(t)$ has to satisfy a two-scale relation (sometimes called the dilation equation or the multi-resolution analysis (MRA) equation) (Rao and Bopardikar 1998, Strang and Nguyen 1997).

$$\phi(t) = 2 \sum_k h(k)\phi(2t - k) \qquad (A7.13)$$

where $h(k)$ is the unit impulse response, k being an integer.

This means that $\phi(t)$ can be expressed in terms of a weighted sum of shifted $\phi(2t)$.

Eq (A7.13) can be written as

$$\phi(t/2) = 2 \sum_k h(k)\phi(t - k) \qquad (A7.14)$$

Taking Fourier Transform of Eq (A7.14) will yield the frequency domain equivalent of the two-scale relation

$$\Phi(2\omega) = H(\omega)\Phi(\omega) \qquad (A7.15)$$

which can be rewritten as

$$H(\omega) = \frac{\Phi(2\omega)}{\Phi(\omega)} \qquad (A7.16)$$

Using Eq (A7.12), $H(\omega)$ can be written as

$$H(\omega) = \begin{cases} 1 & |\omega| \leq \dfrac{\pi}{2} \\ 0 & \dfrac{\pi}{2} < |\omega| \leq \pi \end{cases} \qquad (A7.17)$$

which is an ideal low pass filter with cutoff frequency $\pi/2$.

Its inverse Fourier Transform (see Eq (A2.15)), which is the coefficients of the ideal low pass filter, is given by (Strang and Nguyen 1997, p45)

$$h(k) = \frac{\sin \dfrac{\pi k}{2}}{\pi k} = \begin{cases} 1/2 & k = 0 \\ \pm 1/(\pi k) & k \text{ odd} \\ 0 & k \text{ even}, k \neq 0 \end{cases}$$

$$= \begin{cases} 1/2 & k = 0 \\ 1/(\pi k) & k = \pm 1, \pm 5, ... \\ -1/(\pi k) & k = \pm 3, \pm 7, ... \\ 0 & k \text{ even}, k \neq 0 \end{cases} \qquad (A7.18)$$

The sinc function is thus a scaling function, and it is needed to derive the corresponding wavelet.

But first, an ideal highpass filter $H_1(\omega)$ needs to be constructed. It is orthogonal to the ideal lowpass filter $H(\omega)$, as we can simply set $H_1 = 1$ in the interval where $H = 0$ (Strang and Nguyen 1997)

$$H_1(\omega) = \begin{cases} 0 & |\omega| \le \pi/2 \\ 1 & \pi/2 < |\omega| \le \pi \end{cases}$$ (A7.19)

Its inverse Fourier Transform, which is the coefficient of the ideal high pass filter is given by

$$h_1(k) = \frac{\sin \pi k}{\pi k} - \frac{\sin \dfrac{\pi k}{2}}{\pi k} = \begin{cases} 1/2 & k = 0 \\ \mp 1/(\pi k) & k \text{ odd} \\ 0 & k \text{ even}, k \ne 0 \end{cases}$$

$$= \begin{cases} 1/2 & k = 0 \\ -1/(\pi k) & k = \pm 1, \pm 5, ... \\ 1/(\pi k) & k = \pm 3, \pm 7, ... \\ 0 & k \text{ even}, k \ne 0 \end{cases}$$ (A7.20)

The wavelet $\psi(t)$ is given by one application of the high pass filter (with downsampling) to $\phi(t)$ (Strang and Nguyen 1997, p52; Rao and Bopardikar 1998, p71).

$$\psi(t) = 2 \sum_k h_1(k)\phi(2t - k)$$ (A7.21)

Fourier Transform of Eq (A7.21) is given by

$$\Psi(\omega)=H_1\left(\frac{\omega}{2}\right)\Phi\left(\frac{\omega}{2}\right)=\begin{cases}1 & \text{for } \pi<|\omega|\leq 2\pi \\ 0 & \text{otherwise}\end{cases} \qquad (A7.22)$$

Its inverse Fourier Transform, $\psi(t)$, is the sinc wavelet

$$\psi(t)=\frac{\sin 2\pi t}{\pi t}-\frac{\sin \pi t}{\pi t} \qquad (A7.23)$$

This is called the mother wavelet from which a class of expansion functions $\psi_{j,k}(t)$ can be generated (Burrus et al 1998)

$$\psi_{j,k}(t) = 2^{j/2}\psi(2^j t - k) = 2^{j/2}\psi[2^j(t-2^{-j}k)] \qquad (A7.24)$$

where j, k are integers. 2^j is the scaling of t. $2^{-j}k$ is the translation in t. $2^{j/2}$ maintains the norm of the wavelet at different scales, such that

$$\int_{-\infty}^{\infty}\psi_{j,k}(t)\,\psi_{\ell,m}(t)\,dt=\delta_{j\ell}\delta_{km} \qquad (A7.25)$$

$$\text{where } \delta_{j\ell}=\begin{cases}1 & \text{when } j=\ell \\ 0 & \text{when } j\neq\ell\end{cases} \qquad (A7.26)$$

Thus, $\psi_{j,k}(t)$ forms an orthonormal basis. Any function f(t) can be written as (Burrus et al 1998)

$$f(t) = \sum_k c_{j_0}(k)\phi_{j_0,k}(t) + \sum_k \sum_{j=j_0}^{\infty} d_j(k)\psi_{j,k}(t) \qquad (A7.27)$$

where $\phi_{j_0,k}(t) = 2^{j_0/2}\phi(2^{j_0}t - k)$ $\qquad (A7.28)$

The coefficients in this wavelet expansion are called the discrete wavelet transform (DWT) of the signal f(t). They are similar to the Fourier series expansion in the Fourier Analysis. These wavelet coefficients can be calculated by inner products

$$c_{j_0}(k) = \langle f(t), \phi_{j_0,k}(t) \rangle = \int f(t)\phi_{j_0,k}(t)dt \qquad (A7.29)$$

and

$$d_j(k) = \langle f(t), \psi_{j,k}(t) \rangle = \int f(t)\psi_{j,k}(t)dt \qquad (A7.30)$$

For any practical signal that is bandlimited, there will be an upper scale j = J, above which the wavelet coefficients, $d_j(k)$, are very small. Thus, a signal f(t) can be written as

$$f(t) = \sum_k c_{j_0}(k)\phi_{j_0,k}(t) + \sum_k \sum_{j=j_0}^{J-1} d_j(k)\psi_{j,k}(t) \qquad (A7.31)$$

Ignoring k (which represents translation in t) in Eq (A7.24), we can write

$$\psi_j(t) = 2^{j/2}\psi(2^j t) \tag{A7.32}$$

For j = -3, -4, -5, the sinc wavelets are

$$\psi_{-3}(t) = 2^{-3/2} \, 8 \left[\frac{\sin\dfrac{\pi t}{4}}{\pi t} - \frac{\sin\dfrac{\pi t}{8}}{\pi t} \right] \tag{A7.33}$$

$$\psi_{-4}(t) = 2^{-2} \, 16 \left[\frac{\sin\dfrac{\pi t}{8}}{\pi t} - \frac{\sin\dfrac{\pi t}{16}}{\pi t} \right] \tag{A7.34}$$

$$\psi_{-5}(t) = 2^{-5/2} \, 32 \left[\frac{\sin\dfrac{\pi t}{16}}{\pi t} - \frac{\sin\dfrac{\pi t}{32}}{\pi t} \right] \tag{A7.35}$$

Ignoring the numerical factor on the RHS, the Fourier Transform of Eq (A7.33) – (A7.35) are

$$\Psi\left\{\frac{\sin\dfrac{\pi t}{4}}{\pi t}-\frac{\sin\dfrac{\pi t}{8}}{\pi t}\right\}=\begin{cases}1 & \pi/8<|\omega|\leq\pi/4 \\ 0 & \text{otherwise}\end{cases} \qquad (A7.36)$$

$$\Psi\left\{\frac{\sin\dfrac{\pi t}{8}}{\pi t}-\frac{\sin\dfrac{\pi t}{16}}{\pi t}\right\}=\begin{cases}1 & \pi/16<|\omega|\leq\pi/8 \\ 0 & \text{otherwise}\end{cases} \qquad (A7.37)$$

$$\Psi\left\{\frac{\sin\dfrac{\pi t}{16}}{\pi t}-\frac{\sin\dfrac{\pi t}{32}}{\pi t}\right\}=\begin{cases}1 & \pi/32<|\omega|\leq\pi/16 \\ 0 & \text{otherwise}\end{cases} \qquad (A7.38)$$

Thus, wavelets are essentially bandpass filters. They are called "constant-Q" filters as the ratio of the band width to the center frequency of the band is constant. It should be noted that in Eq(A7.36) – (A7.38), signals that pass through these bandpass filters do not experience any phase shifts, as there is no imaginary part on the RHS. The Fourier integral in these equations integrate from -∞ to ∞. This, however, cannot be applied to on-line or real-time applications, where only past but not future data exist. In these applications, the integral integrates from 0 to ∞, and the filter is called a causal filter (Strang and Nguyen 1997, Hayes 1999).

The Fourier Transform of a causal low pass filter $[\sin(\omega_0 t)]/(\pi t)$, is given by

$$\int_0^\infty \frac{\sin \omega_0 t}{\pi t} \exp(-i\omega t) dt = \frac{1}{4}\frac{\omega_0 + \omega}{|\omega_0 + \omega|} + \frac{1}{4}\frac{\omega_0 - \omega}{|\omega_0 - \omega|} - i\frac{1}{2\pi}\ell n \frac{|\omega_0 + \omega|}{|\omega_0 - \omega|}$$

$$(A7.39)$$

Thus, the Fourier Transform of a causal band pass filter $[\sin(\omega_0 t)]/(\pi t) - [\sin(\omega_1 t)]/(\pi t)$, where $\omega_1 < \omega_0$, is given by

$$\int_0^\infty \left(\frac{\sin \omega_0 t}{\pi t} - \frac{\sin \omega_1 t}{\pi t} \right) \exp(-i\omega t) dt$$

$$= \frac{1}{4}\frac{\omega_0 + \omega}{|\omega_0 + \omega|} + \frac{1}{4}\frac{\omega_0 - \omega}{|\omega_0 - \omega|} - \frac{1}{4}\frac{\omega_1 + \omega}{|\omega_1 + \omega|} - \frac{1}{4}\frac{\omega_1 - \omega}{|\omega_1 - \omega|}$$

$$+ i\frac{1}{2\pi}\ell n \frac{|\omega_0 - \omega||\omega_1 + \omega|}{|\omega_0 + \omega||\omega_1 - \omega|} \qquad (A7.40)$$

As there is an imaginary part in the RHS of Eq(A7.40), any signal of circular frequency ω, will have a phase shift unless

$$-\frac{(\omega_1 + \omega)(\omega_0 - \omega)}{(\omega_1 - \omega)(\omega_0 + \omega)} = 0 \qquad (A7.41)$$

The negative sign on the LHS of Eq (A7.41) is required for the frequency band $-\omega_0 < \omega < -\omega_1$ and $\omega_1 < \omega < \omega_0$.

Solving Eq (A7.41)

$$\omega = \sqrt{(\omega_1 \omega_0)} \tag{A7.42}$$

For $\omega_1 = \omega_0/2$,

$$\omega = \omega_0/\sqrt{2} \tag{A7.43}$$

Table A7.1 lists the higher frequency ω_0 and lower frequency ω_1 of the sinc band pass filters which will ensure zero phase shift of a signal at circular frequency ω.

Table A7.1.

	ω_1	ω	ω_0
ψ_{-3}	$\pi/8$	$\pi/(4\sqrt{2})$	$\pi/4$
ψ_{-4}	$\pi/16$	$\pi/(8\sqrt{2})$	$\pi/8$
ψ_{-5}	$\pi/32$	$\pi(16\sqrt{2})$	$\pi/16$

The wavelets corresponding to the band pass filters described in Eq (A7.33) – (A7.35) has a continuous variable t. They have to be changed to discrete filters in order to convolute with the discrete data. Writing t = kΔt where Δt is one unit of time interval, which can be a 5 minutes, 15 minutes, etc., t can be changed to k. Furthermore, the constant factors on the RHS of Eq (A7.33) – (A7.35) should be ignored. The coefficients corresponding to the discrete band pass filters can be written as

$$h_{-3}(k) = \frac{1}{\pi k} \left[\sin \frac{\pi k}{4} - \sin \frac{\pi k}{8} \right] \tag{A7.44}$$

$$h_{-4}(k) = \frac{1}{\pi k}\left[\sin\frac{\pi k}{8} - \sin\frac{\pi k}{16}\right] \qquad (A7.45)$$

$$h_{-5}(k) = \frac{1}{\pi k}\left[\sin\frac{\pi k}{16} - \sin\frac{\pi k}{32}\right] \qquad (A7.46)$$

h_{-3}, h_{-4}, h_{-5} are named high, middle and low wavelet indicator in this book. The h's in Eqs (A7.44) – (A7.46) are different from the h in Eq (A7-13) and h_1 in Eq (A7.20). While they are all unit impulse responses, they correspond to different filters. h_{-3} in Eq (A7.44) is plotted in Fig. 9.1. The amplitude and phase of its Fourier Transform are plotted in Figs. A7.1(a) and (b). h_{-4} in Eq (A7.45) is plotted in Fig. 9.2. The amplitude and phase of its Fourier Transform are plotted in Figs. A7.2(a) and (b). h_{-5} in Eq (A7.46) is plotted in Fig. 9.3. The amplitude and phase of its Fourier Transform are plotted in Figs. A7.3(a) and (b). It should be noted that the circular frequencies where the phases are zero in Fig. A7.1(b), Fig. A7.2(b) and Fig. A7.3(b) agree quite well with that shown in Table A7.1.

Figure 9.5 plots a 5-minute chart of an US 30 year Treasury Bond Future. $v*h_{-3}$, $v*h_{-4}$ and $v*h_{-5}$ were employed to convolute with the closing price data and were plotted as a thick line, middle thick line and a thin line respectively in the middle plot., v being the cubic velocity indicator. The bottom plot plots

$$(v*h_{-3} + v*h_{-4} + v*h_{-5}) * x = v*(h_{-3} + h_{-4} + h_{-5}) * x \qquad (A7.47)$$

where x is the closing price data. $h_{-3} + h_{-4} + h_{-5}$ is equivalent to a band pass filter which will transmit circular frequency from $\pi/32$ to $\pi/4$ radian.

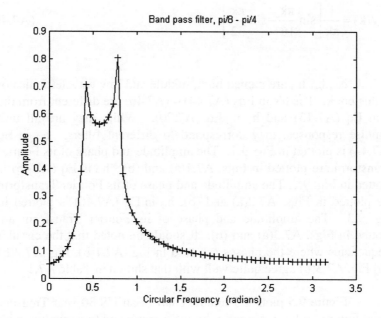

Fig. A7.1(a). Amplitude response of high wavelet indicator.

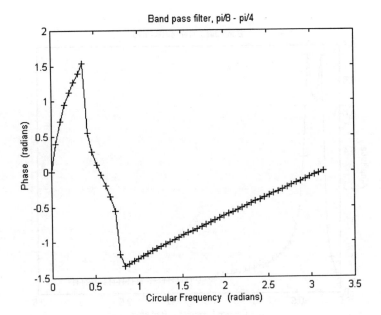

Fig. A7.1(b). Phase response of high wavelet indicator.

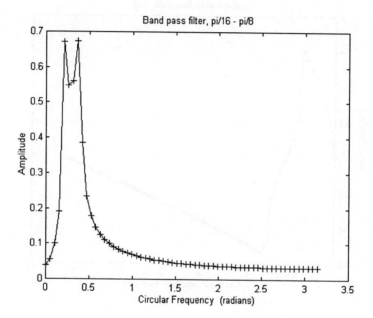

Fig. A7.2(a). Amplitude response of middle wavelet indicator.

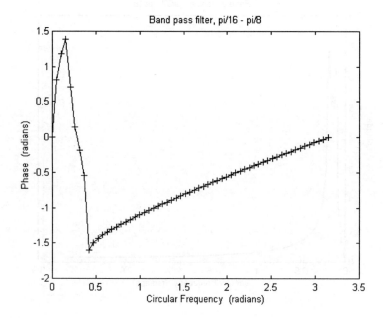

Fig. A7.2(b). Phase response of middle wavelet indicator.

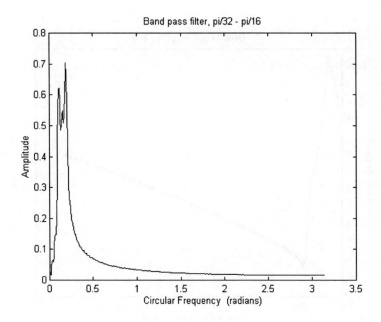

Fig. A7.3(a). Amplitude response of low wavelet indicator.

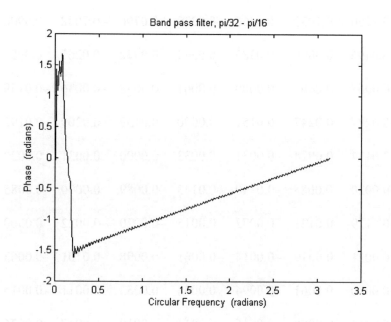

Fig. A7.3(b). Phase response of low wavelet indicator.

A7.3 Coefficients of the Sinc Wavlet Indicators

The indicator coefficients h_{-3}, h_{-4} and h_{-5} are listed below. The first row of each h corresponds to k = 0, 1, 2, 3 ....

$h_{-3} =$

0.1250	0.1033	0.0466	−0.0230	−0.0796	−0.1038	−0.0906
−0.0496	0.0000	0.0385	0.0543	0.0472	0.0265	0.0053
−0.0067	−0.0069	0.0000	0.0061	0.0052	−0.0036	−0.0159
−0.0247	−0.0247	−0.0151	0.0000	0.0139	0.0209	0.0192
0.0114	0.0024	−0.0031	−0.0033	0.0000	0.0031	0.0027
−0.0020	−0.0088	−0.0140	−0.0143	−0.0089	0.0000	0.0085
0.0129	0.0121	0.0072	0.0015	−0.0020	−0.0022	0.0000
0.0021	0.0019	−0.0014	−0.0061	−0.0098	−0.0101	−0.0063
0.0000	0.0061	0.0094	0.0088	0.0053	0.0011	−0.0015
−0.0016	0.0000	0.0016	0.0014	−0.0010	−0.0047	−0.0075
−0.0078	−0.0049	0.0000	0.0048	0.0073	0.0069	0.0042
0.0009	−0.0012	−0.0013	0.0000	0.0013	0.0011	−0.0008
−0.0038	−0.0061	−0.0063	−0.0040	0.0000	0.0039	0.0060
0.0057	0.0035	0.0007	−0.0010	−0.0011	0.0000	0.0011
0.0010	−0.0007	−0.0032	−0.0051	−0.0053	−0.0034	0.0000
0.0033	0.0051	0.0049	0.0029	0.0006	−0.0008	−0.0009

0.0000   0.0009   0.0008   −0.0006   −0.0027   −0.0044   −0.0046

−0.0029   0.0000

$h_{-4} =$

0.0625   0.0597   0.0516   0.0391   0.0233   0.0059   −0.0115

−0.0272   −0.0398   −0.0482   −0.0519   −0.0508   −0.0453   −0.0362

−0.0248   −0.0123   0.0000   0.0108   0.0193   0.0248   0.0272

0.0266   0.0236   0.0189   0.0133   0.0076   0.0027   −0.0011

−0.0033   −0.0040   −0.0034   −0.0019   0.0000   0.0018   0.0030

0.0033   0.0026   0.0008   −0.0018   −0.0049   −0.0080   −0.0106

−0.0124   −0.0130   −0.0123   −0.0105   −0.0075   −0.0039   0.0000

0.0038   0.0069   0.0092   0.0104   0.0105   0.0096   0.0079

0.0057   0.0033   0.0012   −0.0005   −0.0016   −0.0019   −0.0017

−0.0009   0.0000   0.0009   0.0016   0.0017   0.0014   0.0004

−0.0010   −0.0027   −0.0044   −0.0059   −0.0070   −0.0074   −0.0071

−0.0061   −0.0044   −0.0023   0.0000   0.0023   0.0042   0.0057

0.0065   0.0066   0.0060   0.0050   0.0036   0.0021   0.0008

−0.0003   −0.0010   −0.0013   −0.0011   −0.0006   0.0000   0.0006

0.0011   0.0012   0.0009   0.0003   −0.0007   −0.0018   −0.0031

−0.0041 −0.0049 −0.0052 −0.0050 −0.0043 −0.0032 −0.0017

0.0000   0.0016   0.0030   0.0041   0.0047   0.0048   0.0044

0.0036   0.0027

$h_{-5} =$

0.0312   0.0309   0.0299   0.0281   0.0258   0.0229   0.0195

0.0158   0.0117   0.0073   0.0029 −0.0015 −0.0058 −0.0098

−0.0136 −0.0170 −0.0199 −0.0223 −0.0241 −0.0253 −0.0260

−0.0260 −0.0254 −0.0243 −0.0226 −0.0206 −0.0181 −0.0154

−0.0124 −0.0093 −0.0061 −0.0030   0.0000   0.0028   0.0054

0.0077   0.0096   0.0112   0.0124   0.0132   0.0136   0.0136

0.0133   0.0127   0.0118   0.0107   0.0094   0.0081   0.0066

0.0052   0.0038   0.0025   0.0013   0.0003 −0.0005 −0.0012

−0.0017 −0.0019 −0.0020 −0.0019 −0.0017 −0.0014 −0.0010

−0.0005   0.0000   0.0005   0.0009   0.0013   0.0015   0.0017

0.0017   0.0016   0.0013   0.0009   0.0004 −0.0002 −0.0009

−0.0017 −0.0024 −0.0032 −0.0040 −0.0047 −0.0053 −0.0058

−0.0062 −0.0064 −0.0065 −0.0064 −0.0062 −0.0058 −0.0052

−0.0046 −0.0038 −0.0029 −0.0020 −0.0010   0.0000   0.0010

0.0019	0.0027	0.0035	0.0041	0.0046	0.0050	0.0052
0.0053	0.0053	0.0051	0.0048	0.0044	0.0039	0.0034
0.0028	0.0023	0.0017	0.0011	0.0006	0.0001	–0.0002
–0.0006	–0.0008	–0.0009	–0.0010	–0.0009	–0.0008	–0.0007
–0.0005	–0.0002	0.0000	0.0002	0.0005	0.0006	0.0008
0.0009	0.0009	0.0008	0.0007	0.0005	0.0002	–0.0001
–0.0005	–0.0009	–0.0013	–0.0018	–0.0022	–0.0026	–0.0030
–0.0033	–0.0035	–0.0037	–0.0037	–0.0037	–0.0036	–0.0034
–0.0031	–0.0027	–0.0022	–0.0017	–0.0012	–0.0006	0.0000
0.0006	0.0011	0.0017	0.0021	0.0025	0.0028	0.0031
0.0032	0.0033	0.0033	0.0032	0.0030	0.0028	0.0025
0.0022	0.0018	0.0014	0.0011	0.0007	0.0004	0.0001
–0.0002	–0.0004	–0.0005	–0.0006	–0.0006	–0.0006	–0.0005
–0.0004	–0.0003	–0.0002	0.0000	0.0002	0.0003	0.0004
0.0005	0.0006	0.0006	0.0006	0.0005		

A7.4 Other Wavelets

In this book, only sinc wavelets have been introduced to analyze market data. Many different kinds of wavelets have been constructed (Von Baeyer 1995, Strang 1994). The analysis wavelet should be carefully matched to the phenomenon of interest so as to bring out the significant information in the signal (Trevino and

Andreas 1996).   Other wavelets, especially ones with fast decay, should be investigated in the future.

Furthermore, scaling functions are actually low pass filters. They can be employed as powerful trending indicators.

Appendix 8

Skipped Convolution and Forecasting

The mathematical details of skipped convolution and forecasting are described below.

A8.1 Skipped Convolution

Skipped convolution can be defined as

$$y_M(m) = \sum_k h(k)\, x(m - Mk) \tag{A8.1}$$

The financial data are skipped in a larger time frame interval and then analyzed. When $M = 1$, Eq (A8.1) will reduce back to the conventional convolution, i. e., $y_1 = y$, with y given by Eq (A2.6).

When $m = Mn$, the result would be the same as downsampling the data, i.e. $(\downarrow M)\mathbf{x}$ and then convolute the downsampled data with the filter h. Downsampling $\mathbf{x}$ will yield

$$\mathbf{v} = (\downarrow M)\mathbf{x} \tag{A8.2}$$

$$v(n) = [(\downarrow M)\mathbf{x}](n) = x(Mn) \tag{A8.3}$$

Performing convolution on downsampled x yields

$$y = h * v = h * (\downarrow M)\mathbf{x} \tag{A8.4}$$

which can also be written as

$$y(n) = \sum_k h(k)\, v(n-k) \qquad\qquad\qquad (A8.5)$$

When m = Mn, the skipped convolution yields

$$y_M(m) = y_M(Mn) = \sum_k h(k)\, x(Mn - Mk)$$

$$= \sum_k h(k)\, x\,[M(n-k)] = \sum_k h(k)\, v(n-k) = y(n) \qquad (A8.6)$$

Eq (A8.6) can be re-written as

$$\mathbf{y} = (\!\downarrow\! M)\mathbf{y}_M \qquad\qquad\qquad\qquad (A8.7)$$

For example, if y is an indicator in the 15-minute chart, and y_M is the same indicator in the 5-minute chart, and M = 3,

$$y_M(3n) = y(n) \qquad\qquad\qquad\qquad (A8.8)$$

      If a certain market action (as illustrated by the indicator response) arrives at $y_M(3n)$ in the 5-minute chart, then it will be exactly the same as y(n) in the 15-minute chart. However, if the market action arrives at $y_M(3n-1)$ or $y_M(3n-2)$ in the 5-minute chart, then the trader will know 5 or 10 minutes ahead of other traders using a 15-minute chart. Thus, the skipped convolution has a definite advantage.

A8.2 Forecasting

To forecast in a time series, different techniques can be used. One technique is to use the minimum mean square error forecasts in time series analysis (Box, Jenkins and Reinsel 1994). Another technique is to assume that the time series is generated by a frequency band limited process and to forecast future values by using Shannon's sampling theorem (Santana and Mendes 1992).

In this book, we use a different technique by making use of a theorem which states that a function $x(t)$ can be written in a Taylor series (Kaplan 1959)

$$x(t) = \sum_{m=0}^{\infty} c_m (t - t_0)^m \qquad (A8.9)$$

where

$$c_0 = x(t_0), \quad c_1 = x'(t_0), \quad c_2 = (1/2)x''(t_0), \quad .... \qquad (A8.10)$$

x' and x'' are the first and second derivatives of x with respect to t.

Taking t_0 to be the present time, t will be the future time. If we take $t-t_0$ to be one time bar, then $x(t)$ will be the one-step-ahead forecast of the market value. Approximating $x(t)$ to be the sum of the first two terms only, we get

$$x(t) = x(t_0) + x'(t_0) \qquad (A8.11)$$

As the output response of the cubic velocity indicator given by Eq (6.5) approximates the first derivative, the one-step-ahead forecast $x(t)$ can be written as

$$x(1) = x(0) + (11/6)x(0) - 3x(-1) + (3/2)x(-2) - (1/3)x(-3)$$

$$= (17/6)x(0) - 3x(-1) + (3/2)x)(-2) + (1/3)x(-3) \qquad \text{(A8.12)}$$

If we approximate $x(t)$ to be the sum of the first three terms of Eq (A8.9), we get

$$x(t) = x(t_0) + x'(t_0) + (1/2)x''(t_0) \qquad \text{(A8.13)}$$

As the output response of the cubic acceleration indicator given by Eq(6.7) approximates the second derivative, the one-step-ahead forecast can be written as

$$x(1) = x(0) + (11/6)x(0) - 3x(-1) + (3/2)x(-2) - (1/3)x(-3)$$
$$+ (1/2)[2x(0) - 5x(-1) + 4x(-2) - x(-3)]$$

$$= (23/6)x(0) - (11/2)x(-1) + (7/2)x(-2) - (5/6)x(-3) \qquad \text{(A8.14)}$$

Bibliography

Aris, R., *Mathematical Modelling Techniques*, Dover Publications, Inc. (1994).

Ayres, F., Jr., *Schaum's First Year College Mathematics*, McGraw-Hill (1958).

Beckman, R. C., *Powertiming, Using the Elliott Wave Systems to Anticipate and Time Market Turns*, Probus Publishing Company (1992).

Box, G. E. P., Jenkins, G. M. and Reinsel, G. C., *Time Series Analysis — Forecasting and Control*, Prentice-Hall (1994).

Brigham, E. O., *The Fast Fourier Transform*, Prentice-Hall (1974).

Brock, W. A., Hsieh, D. A. and Lebaron, B., *Nonlinear Dynamics, Chaos and Instability: Statistical Theory and Economic Evidence*, MIT Press (1992).

Brock, W. A. and Sayers, C. L., "Is the business cycle characterized by deterministic chaos?", *J. Monetary Econ.*, **22**, 71–90 (1998).

Brockwell, P. J. and Davis, R. A., *Introduction to Time Series and Forecasting*, Springer (1996).

Broesch, J. D., *Digital Signal Processing Demystified*, LLH Technology Publishing (1997).

Burrus, C. S., Gopinath, R. A. and Guo, H., *Introduction to Wavelets and Wavelet Transforms, A Primer*, Prentice-Hall (1998).

Casti, J. L., *Complexification*, Harper Perennial (1995).

Casti, J. L., "What if ...," *New Scientist*, **151**(2038), 36–40 (July 13, 1996).

Casti, J. L., "Flight over Wall Street," *New Scientist*, **154**(2078), 38–41 (April 19, 1997a).

Casti, J. L., *Would-Be Worlds*, John Wiley & Sons, Inc. (1997b).

Capobianco, E., "Statistical analysis of financial volatility by wavelet shrinkage," *Methodology and Computing in Applied Probability*, **1**, 423–443 (1999).

Chorafas, D. N., *Chaos Theory in the Financial Markets*, Probus Publishing Company (1994).

DeMark, T. R., *The New Science of Technical Analysis*, John Wiley & Sons, Inc. (1994).

Ehlers, J. F., *MESA and Trading Market Cycles*, John Wiley & Sons (1992).

Elder, A., *Trading for a Living*, John Wiley & Sons (1993).

Fishman, M. B., Barr, D. S. and Leick, W. J., "Using neural nets in market analysis," *Technical Analysis of Stocks and Commodities*, **9**, 18–20 (1991).

Freund, J. E., *Mathematical Statistics*, Prentice Hall (1992).

Gilmore, C. G., "A new approach to testing for chaos, with applications in finance and economics," *Complexity and Chaos, World Scientific*, 99–103 (1992).

Gleick, J., *Chaos, Making a New Science*, Penguin books (1987).

Hamming, R. W., *Digital Filters*, Third Edition, Dover Publications (1989).

Hatamian, Tim, "Price forecasting I : Linear prediction," *AI in Finance*, 48–54 (Fall 1995).

Hatamian, Tim, "Price forecasting III : Nonlinear prediction," *AI in Finance*, 18–25 (Winter 1996).

Hayes, M. H., *Digital Signal Processing, Schaum's Outlines*, McGraw-Hill (1999).

Hirabayashi, T., Takayasu, H., Miura, H. and Hamada, K., "The behavior of a threshold model of market price in stock exchange," *Fractals*, **1**, 29–40 (1993).

Hubbard, B. B., *The World according to Wavelets*, Second Edition, A. K. Peters, Ltd. (1998).

Jaditz, T. and Sayers, C. L., "Is chaos generic in economic data?", *Complexity and Chaos,World Scientific*, 261–271 (1992).

Kaplan, D. T., "A Geometrical Statistics for detecting deterministic dynamics," *Time Series Prediction: Forecasting the Future and Understanding the Past*, Eds. Weigend, A. S. and Gershenfeld, N. A., pp. 415–428, Addison-Wesley (1994).

Kaplan, W., *Advanced Calculus*, Addison-Wesley (1959).

Lau, K. M. and Weng, H., "Climate signal detection using wavelet transform : How to make a time series sing," *Bulletin of the American Meterological Society*, **76**, 2391–2402 (1995).

Lyons, R. G., *Understanding Digital Signal Processing*, Addison-Wesley (1997).

Mandelbrot, B. B., *The Fractal Geometry of Nature*, W. H. Freeman and Company (1983).

Mandelbrot, B. B., *Fractals and Scaling in Finance*, Springer (1997).

Mantegna, R. N. and Stanley, H. E., "Stochastic process with ultraslow convergence to a Gaussian: The truncated Levy flight," *Physical Review Letters*, **73**, 2946–2949 (1994).

Mantegna, R. N. and Stanley, H. E., "Scaling behaviour in the dynamics of an economic index," *Nature*, **376**, 46–49 (1995).

McNeill, D. and Freiberger, P., *Fuzzy Logic*, Simon & Schuster (1993).

Mesterton-Gibbons, *A Concrete Approach to Mathematical Modelling*, John Wiley & Sons, Inc. (1995).

Meyer, P. L., *Introductory Probability and Statistical Applications*, Addison-Wesley (1965).

Neely, G., *Mastering Elliott Wave*, Winsor Books (1990).

Oppenheim, A. V., Schafer, R. W., with Buck, J. R., *Discrete-Time Signal Processing*, Second Edition, Prentice-Hall (1999).

Palmer, R. G., Arthur, W. B., Holland, J. H., LeBaron, B. and Tayler, P., "Artificial economic life: A simple model of a stockmarket," *Physica D*, **75**, 264–274 (1994).

Peitgen, P. H. and Richter, P. H., *The Beauty of Fractals: Images of Complex Dynamical Systems*, Springer-Verlag (1998).

Peterson, I., *The Jungles of Randomness, a Mathematical Safari*, John Wiley & Sons, Inc (1997).

Pincus, S., "Approximate entropy as a measure of system complexity," *Proceedings of National Academy of Sciences of the USA*, **88**, 2297–2301 (1991).

Pincus, S., "Approximate entropy (ApEn) as a complexity measure," *Chaos*, **5**, 110–117 (1995).

Pincus, S. and Singer, B. H., "Randomness and degrees of irregularity," *Proceedings of National Academy of Sciences of the USA*, **93**, 2083–2088 (1996).

Pincus, S. and Kalman, R. E., "Not all (possibly) 'random' sequences are created equal," *Proceedings of National Academy of Sciences of the USA*, **94**, 3513–3518 (1997).

Plummer, T., *Forecasting Financial Markets*, John Wiley & Sons (1990).

Prechter Jr., R. R. and Frost, A. J., *Elliott Wave Principle*, New Classic Library (1990).

Pring, M. J., *Technical Analysis Explained, The Successful Investor's Guide to Spotting Investment Trends and Turning Points*, Third Edition, McGraw-Hill Inc. (1991).

Proakis, J. G. and Manolakis, D. G., *Digital Signal Processing, Principles, Algorithms and Applications*, Third Edition, Prentice-Hall (1996).

Protter, M. H. and Morrey, C. B., Jr., *Calculus with Analytic Geometry*, Addison-Wesley (1963).

Ramsey, J. B., Usikov, D. and Zaslavsky, G. M., "An analysis of U.S. stock price behavior using wavelets," *Fractals*, **3**, 377–389 (1995).

Ramsey, J. B. and Lampart, C., "Decomposition of economic relationships by time scale using wavelets : Money and income," *Macroecon. Dynam.*, **2**, 49–71 (1998a).

Ramsey, J. B. and Lampart, C., "Decomposition of economic relationships by time scale using wavelets : Expenditure and income," *Stud. Nonlinear Dynam. Econometrics*, **3**, 23–42 (1998b).

Ramsey, J. B., "The contribution of wavelets to the analysis of economic and financial data," *Phil. Trans. of the Royal Society Lond. A*, **357**, 2593–2606 (1999).

Rao, R. M. and Bopardikar, A. S., *Wavelet Transforms, Introduction to Theory and Applications*, Addison-Wesley (1998).

Santana, J. and Mendes, R. V., "Prediction of time series," *Complexity in Physics and Technology*, pp. 263–280, World Scientific (1992).

Sherald, M. and Ward, S., "Market predictions with backprop neural nets," *AI in Finance*, 25–31 (Fall 1994).

Shin, T. and Han, I., "Optimal multi-scale time series decomposition for financial forecasting using wavelet thresholding techniques," Lecture Notes in Artificial Intelligence, *Proceedings of the 7ᵗʰ International Workshop of New Directions in Rough Sets, Data Mining and Granular-Soft Computing, RSFDGrC'99*, pp. 533–542 (1999).

Sowell, T., *Fuzzy Logic for "Just Plain Folks" — Plug in to the Systems Control, Financial and Emotional Success Genius Born in You*, Tesco Publishing Co. (1998).

Stewart, I., "Putting randomness in order," *New Scientist*, **154**(2081), 22 (May 10, 1997).

Strang, G., "Wavelets," *American Scientist*, **82**, 250–255 (1994).

Strang, G. and Nguyen, T., *Wavelets and Filter Banks*, Wellesley-Cambridge Press, (Revised Edition) (1997).

Trevino, G. and Andreas, E. L., "On wavelet analysis of nonstationary turbulence," *Boundary-Layer Meteorology*, **81**, 271–188 (1996).

Valdez-Cepeda, R. D. and Solano-Herrera, E., "Self-affinity of records of financial indexes," *Fractals*, **7**, 427–432 (1999).

Von Baeyer, H. C. V., "Wave of the future," *Discover*, **16**, 69–74 (1995).

Waldrop, M. M., *Complexity*, Simon & Schuster (1992).

Weigend, A. S. and Gershenfeld, *Time Series Prediction: Forecasting the Future and Understanding the Past*, Addison-Wesley Publishing Company (1994).

Weinstein, S., *Secrets for Profiting in Bull and Bear Markets*, Business One Irwin (1988).

Zweig, M. E., *Winning on Wall Street*, Warner Books (1990).

Index